Pied Piper of Atheism

PETE VERE
and
SANDRA MIESEL

Pied Piper of Atheism

Philip Pullman and Children's Fantasy

IGNATIUS PRESS   SAN FRANCISCO

Cover design by John Herreid

© 2007 by Ignatius Press, San Francisco
All rights reserved
ISBN 978-1-58617-255-8
Library of Congress Control Number 2007941452
Printed in the United States of America ∞

CONTENTS

Introduction

Pullman's Puzzling Philosophy

Carl E. Olson

There is, I think, much to like about British novelist Philip Pullman. He has a dry wit that is often self-deprecating. He laments the drudgery of mass-induced "learning" at the expense of reading great literature. His love for good writing is apparent and sincere. And even his critics—including the authors of this book—acknowledge that he is an imaginative and talented author.

Numerous readers of all ages have certainly taken a liking to the sixty-something (b. 1946) writer's *His Dark Materials* trilogy, which has now sold over ten million copies. And the critics cannot get enough. Books in the series have garnered many prestigious awards, including the 1995 Carnegie Medal for *Northern Lights* (released as *The Golden*

Compass in North America). *Northern Lights* was also selected in 2007 as one of the Carnegie Anniversary Top Ten books of the past seventy years.[1] The third book, *The Amber Spyglass*, won both the prestigious 2001 Whitbread Prize for best children's book and the Whitbread Book of the Year prize in 2002, being the first children's book to win the award. And, of course, *The Golden Compass* is now a major motion picture, produced by New Line Cinema, released in early December 2007.

His Dark Materials describes and celebrates a world without religion and with no need for God. The trilogy, Pullman stated in an interview with Random House, "depicts a struggle: the old forces of control and ritual and authority, the forces which have been embodied throughout human history in such phenomena as the Inquisition, the witch-trials, [and] the burning of heretics, and which are still strong today in the regions of the world where religious zealots of any faith have power, are on one side; and the forces that fight against them have as their guiding principle an idea which is summed up in the words The Republic of Heaven. It's the

[1] http://www.cilip.org.uk/aboutcilip/newsandpressreleases/news070622.htm (accessed December 10, 2007).

Kingdom against the Republic."[2] Pullman explains that the books depict temptation and the Fall not as "the source of all woe and misery, as in traditional Christian teaching, but as the beginning of true human freedom something to be celebrated, not lamented". The "Tempter is not an evil being like Satan," he contends, "but a figure who might stand for Wisdom."

Pullman has made it known he is not against "the religious impulse", which, he writes on his website (www.philip-pullman.com), "includes the sense of awe and mystery we feel when we look at the universe, the urge to find a meaning and a purpose in our lives, our sense of moral kinship with other human beings."[3] Rather, he hates "organized religion", which he equates primarily with churches, priesthoods, sacred scriptures, an invisible god, and objective truth. These characteristics are connected, in Pullman's view, with routine acts of violence, torture, and slavery imposed upon "millions" of people. In a November/December 2002 interview with *Book Magazine*, he said, "I'm for

[2] Random House Q & A with Philip Pullman, http://www.randomhouse.com/features/pullman/author/qa.html (accessed November 26, 2007).

[3] "About the Worlds: Religion", http://www.philip-pullman.com/pages/content/index.asp?PageID=12 (accessed November 29, 2007).

open-mindedness and tolerance. I'm against any
form of fanaticism, fundamentalism or zealotry, and
this certainty of 'We have the truth.' The truth is
far too large and complex. Nobody has the truth." [4]
But how can such a statement be true if no one
has the truth? Further confusing matters is a remark
made by Pullman during a March 2004 public dialogue with Dr. Rowan Williams, the archbishop
of Canterbury and the head of the Anglican Com-
munion: "I'm temperamentally 'agin' [against] the
post modernist position that there is no truth and
it depends on where you are and it's all a result of
the capitalist, imperialist hegemony of the bour-
geois . . . all this sort of stuff. I'm agin that but I
couldn't tell you why." [5]

When Pullman discusses literature and writing,
he displays the knowledge gained from many years
spent reading fiction and from teaching English literature at Oxford. But his remarks about religion,
focused mostly on Christianity, are broad, simplis-
tic, and lacking the sort of detail that might suggest

[4] Anna Weinberg, "Are You There, God? It's Me, Philip Pullman"
(*Book Magazine*, November–December 2002), p. 11.

[5] "The Dark Materials Debate: Life, God, the Universe . . .", edited
transcript of a Platform at the National Theatre, *Telegraph*, March 17,
2004, http://www.telegraph.co.uk/arts/main.jhtml?xml=/arts/2004/
03/17/bodark17.xml (accessed November 26, 2007).

time spent studying Christian theology or philosophy. He sounds like the proverbial village atheist, spouting darkly and vaguely about the millions killed, the horrors of dogma, the evils of clergy, and the small-mindedness of orthodox believers. In an October 2000 interview with the *Capital Times*, Pullman opined that "the greatest moral advances have been made by religious leaders such as Jesus and the Buddha. And the greatest moral wickedness has been perpetrated by their followers. How many millions of people have been killed in the name of this religion or that one? Burnt, hanged, tortured. It's just extraordinary." [6] No specific examples were given, and the tens of millions murdered in the twentieth century by atheistic regimes went unmentioned.

However, in an essay, "The War on Words", [7] Pullman attempted to argue that modern atheistic, totalitarian governments—including the former Soviet Union—were actually theocracies, stating, "You

[6] *Capital Times*, http://www.madison.com/tct/. An excerpt of the interview can be found in the *Capital Times* archives: Heather Lee Schroeder, "'Spyglass' Author Finds It Impossible to Believe", http://www.madison.com/tct/archives/index.php?archAction=arch_read&a_from=search&a_file=%2Ftct%2F2000%2F10%2F13%2F0010130332.php&var_search=Search&keyword_field=pullman&pub_code_field=tct&from_date_field=&to_date_field=&var_start_pos=0&var_articles_per_page=10 (accessed November 26, 2007).

[7] *The Guardian*, November 6, 2004; http://books.guardian.co.uk/review/story/0,,1343733,00.html (accessed December 10, 2007).

don't need a belief in God to have a theocracy."
Like fellow British atheist Christopher Hitchens,
author of *God Is Not Great: How Religion Poisons
Everything*, and American counterpart Sam Harris,
who wrote *The End of Faith: Religion, Terror and the
Future of Reason*, Pullman follows this convenient
but misleading line of reasoning so that he can, as
an atheist, both disavow the horrors wrought by
Communism and align them with belief in God.
This despite the plain meaning of theocracy, which
is from the Greek word *theokratia*, meaning "the rule
of God"! Yet, even with his occasional references
to atheistic totalitarianism and Islam, the real focus
of Pullman's criticisms is clear. In a 2001 interview
on the BBC "Belief" radio program, Pullman
acknowledged that *His Dark Materials* draws heav-
ily from the language and vocabulary of Christianity, with descriptions made up of "parts which the
Catholic church has kindly prepared for us". And,
when asked by the host, Joan Bakewell, "are you
gunning for the Catholic church?" Pullman stated,
"I'm happy to have it in place as a—as a villain." [8]
And journalist Erica Wagner (a fan of Pullman's
work), having interviewed the author in 2000, wrote:

[8] Transcript available on http://darkadamant.betterversion.org/
BBC_Belief_Philip_Pullman.txt.

His "Church" is otherworldly: but the parallels are clear. "I am very suspicious of ceremony, hierarchy, ritual," he says. "It represents the ossification of something that was once genuine. The underlying myth of these three books—the story of the Creation and the Fall—clarifies how the original impulses of great religious teachers are used and perverted and taken as empty banners by people who set up churches." He has, he says, a "deep, deep dislike" of any kind of religious organisation: "if there is any good in it, it comes out of human beings and not out of religious structures." [9]

Pullman admits the great influence of his grandfather, an Anglican priest, telling the *Capital Times*, "I'm a Christian atheist, and I'm a church atheist. And I'm very specifically, because I was brought up in my grandfather's household and he was a Church of England priest when the old prayer book was used, so I'm a 1662 Book of Common Prayer atheist, a Hymns Ancient and Modern atheist, and King James Bible atheist." He acknowledges his debt to that upbringing but says he finds it impossible to believe in God. But like other popular (and popularizing) atheists, many of Pullman's remarks about

[9] "Divinely inspired: Philip Pullman", *The Times*, October 18, 2000. http://www.ericawagner.co.uk/journalism.php?section=journalism2&id=14 (accessed December 10, 2007).

the nature of existence, truth, and God are either conflicted or confusing. He insists that this material world is all that exists, but he speaks in transcendent terms about the need for a "Republic of Heaven", a theme that seems to preoccupy him. In a November 2002 interview with Susan Roberts of Surefish.co.uk, Pullman said, "This is not a Kingdom but a Republic, in which we are all free and equal citizens, with—and this is the important thing—responsibilities. With the responsibility to make this place into a Republic of Heaven for everyone. Not to live in it in a state of perpetual self-indulgence, but to work hard to make this place as good as we possibly can." [10] In the *Capital Times* interview, Pullman said of that utopian republic: "By which I mean it's a place where we're connected to other people by love and joy and delight in the universe and the physical world. And we have to use all the qualities we have—our imagination, our intelligence, our scientific understanding, our appreciation of art, our love for each other and so on—we have to work to use those things, to make the world a better place, which it sorely needs making." Pullman apparently misses the fact that since people,

[10] Susan Roberts, "A Dark Agenda?" Surefish.co.uk, November 2002, http://www.surefish.co.uk/culture/features/pullman_interview.htm (accessed November 26, 2007).

as he essentially admits, are religious and communal by nature, it is only natural that "organized religion" would have an ancient, varied history. And, as noted, he is disingenuous about the fact that modern attempts to establish an atheistic state—whether by the French Revolution or the Bolshevik Revolution—have led to unparalleled violence, injustice, and social chaos. Ironically, the Christian doctrine that Pullman seems to detest so much—original sin—is, as Chesterton noted in *Orthodoxy*, "the only part of Christian theology which can really be proved", as the evidence is all around us. Perhaps if Pullman had a more Catholic taste in his reading, he might appreciate how many brilliant and holy Christians have joyfully grappled with the mysteries of life.

In the end, Pullman protests too much and too poorly. However, the serious defects in his philosophical and theological musings are covered up adroitly in his novels, which were praised by Robert McCrum in the *Observer* for containing "very big ideas fearlessly explored".[11] McCrum also noted that the *His Dark Materials* trilogy is "an ambitious tale inspired by *Paradise Lost* with a radical view of

[11] Robert McCrum, "Not for Children", *Guardian*, October 22, 2000, http://observer.guardian.co.uk/review/story/0,,638057,00.html (accessed November 26, 2007).

religion that may well contain the most subversive message in children's literature in years".

That summarizes well the central reason Pete Vere and Sandra Miesel have undertaken the task of writing *Pied Piper of Atheism*. They recognize, as does Pullman, the powerful influence that stories have on children (and, of course, adults) and how those stories can shape beliefs, perspectives, and morality. Their critiques are firm but are not polemical or reactionary. Rather, they take both Pullman's ideas and the power of fiction seriously and respond accordingly. They agree with Pullman's remark that we all need "some sort of over-arching narrative to live by". They disagree with his insistence that the Christian story that once fulfilled that need "is now either dead or dying".[12] Far from being dead, the Christian story is alive and well, even though Philip Pullman strives to write it off and erase it from the pages of history.

[12] Robert McCrum, "Daemon Geezer", *Observer*, January 27, 2002, http://books.guardian.co.uk/whitbread2001/story/0,11169,640032,00.html (accessed November 26, 2007).

Chapter 1

Philip Pullman
The Pied Piper of Atheism

Pete Vere, J.C.L.

The story of *The Pied Piper of Hamelin* is a favorite of children and parents alike. According to the Brothers Grimm, it begins when the German village of Hamelin suffers a rat infestation. A traveling pipe player promises to rid the village of rodents in exchange for an agreed-upon sum of gold. Desperate, the villagers agree to the piper's bargain.

The musician begins to play his pipe. The tune captivates the rats, who crawl out from under the cottages and follow him to the village square. The pied piper continues playing, leading the rats out of the village and down toward the bank of the Weser River. The rats follow the musician into the river and drown.

The pied piper then returns to the village to collect his pay. The villagers refuse. The musician storms out of the village and promises revenge when the villagers least expect it. That moment will come on a Sunday morning while the villagers are in church.

The piper pulls out his instrument anew. But this tune is somewhat different. It catches the ears of the village's children. They drop their toys, halt their games, and cease their other activities. As the piper works his musical enchantment, the children follow him to the village square. He then leads them up a mountain trail and into a cave that seals shut behind them. The village children are never seen again. Only a lame boy is left behind; he could not follow quickly enough to keep up with the piper's tune.

To this young lad falls the task of hobbling back to Hamelin and informing the villagers of what had happened to his playmates.

There are two morals to this story. The first is that parents must always set a good moral example for their children. The second is that parents must remain ever vigilant of their children's welfare. When parents fail at either task, their children find themselves seduced by worldly influences and subsequently led astray.

The Pied Piper of Atheism

Fast-forward to today, and the pied piper has evolved from a fairy tale into a metaphor. The term "pied piper" now refers to an individual who leads children astray. For the devout Christian parent, Philip Pullman is such a man. Pullman is an avowed atheistic humanist whose disdain for the Christian God and the Catholic Church is well documented.

His most popular work, the *His Dark Materials* trilogy, of which *The Golden Compass* is the first book, tells the story of a twelve-year-old girl who sets off on a quest to overthrow God, the Kingdom of Heaven, and the Church. In Pullman's fictional universe, God is the "bad guy" and those who rebel against Him are the "good guys".

Granted, these are not new sentiments in the history of literature and philosophy. Avowed atheists are found at all levels of academia, the popular media, and government. Yet what makes Pullman more dangerous than other avowed anti-Christian thinkers is the medium through which he promotes his ideas. His are not the dry academic treatises of the ivory basement. Rather, Pullman's dark fairy tales are marketed to children as fantasy literature.

Yet in the excitement over J. K. Rowling's *Harry Potter* and its appropriateness as children's literature—a debate in which orthodox Catholics came down both for and against, at least until Dumbledore fell out of the closet—Pullman's work, which is brazenly anti-God and anti-Christian, somehow snuck past the collective radar of Christian parents.

This is in spite of the many worldly honors garnered by the books. Literary critics hail Pullman as a new J. R. R. Tolkien and C. S. Lewis—and as an even more captivating author than J. K. Rowling. *The Golden Compass* has won England's coveted Carnegie Medal and has earned a spot on the American Library Association's Top Ten Best Books for Young Adults list. Pullman's trilogy has received favorable reviews from such respected publications as the *New York Times Book Review*, *Smithsonian Magazine*, and *Salon.com*.

The Golden Compass (previously released in England as *Northern Lights*) is now showing on the silver screen. The movie stars Nicole Kidman, Eva Gaëlle Green, Daniel Craig, and other Hollywood actors and actresses of note. Already there is talk about adapting the remaining two books—*The Subtle Knife* and *The Amber Spyglass*—to film.

Christian parents—once they become aware of Pullman's trilogy—are horrified by its brazen promotion of atheism. Yet even more shocking for parents is to discover Pullman's books on their children's night table. Pastors, principals, and teachers are just as discomforted to find Pullman's books in the library of their parish school. Because of the wide audience Pullman has gained for his work, many Catholic youth have already come across and read his books.

Hence the importance of parents, pastors, principals, and teachers informing themselves about *The Golden Compass*. Parents are the primary educators of their children. As such, they are responsible for their children's intellectual and spiritual formation. Yet they do not raise their children in a vacuum—they depend upon their pastors and the rest of the Catholic community to assist them in the raising of their children in the Christian faith. Parents recognize that young people are easily impressed by the temptations of the world. Pullman is one such temptation, for he uses the medium of children's fantasy literature to undermine the Christian faith and promote atheism.

As this book will demonstrate, Pullman is truly the pied piper of atheism. Let the Christian parent not be caught unaware like the villagers of Hamelin.

The Setting

The Golden Compass begins with a scenario easily recognized by fans of C. S. Lewis' *Chronicles of Narnia*. A young girl is hiding among the robes hanging in the wardrobe of an old academic. The girl's name is Lyra Belacqua (also known as Lyra Silvertongue), and she is twelve years old.

Lyra is an orphan. She has been adopted by the professors of Jordan College, an all-male institute of higher learning and Oxford University's most prestigious college in Pullman's alternate world. Lyra has very little female influence in her life. She lives amidst Jordan College's students, professors, and support staff. Some find her a pet of sorts, while others avoid her as a little savage foisted upon the college's otherwise serious academic milieu.

Lyra intends to spy on Lord Asriel, the man whom she believes to be her uncle. Lord Asriel shows little interest in spending time with Lyra. As a scholar of Jordan College, Lord Asriel's main concern is raising money for his research in experimental theology. This subject matter loosely corresponds in our world to a cross between the natural sciences and the occult. The reader quickly learns that Lord Asriel spends most of his time in an Arctic laboratory, away from the college and away from Lyra.

Daemons, Gender, and Human Nature

Lyra is not alone in the closet. Fluttering about next to the girl is her daemon, Pantalaimon, nicknamed "Pan" for short. He has taken the form of a talking moth. The reader discovers in due time that a daemon is a hybrid of a person's spirit, conscience, and personality. Every human in Pullman's universe possesses a daemon—a personal Jiminy Cricket to accompany the puppets of the world. The daemon takes the form of an animal. Among children the form is always changing from animal to animal, depending upon the child's mood. The daemon's form becomes fixed sometime during the child's adolescence. The daemon dissipates upon death.

The name "daemon" is borrowed from the ancient Greeks. The philosopher Socrates described his daemon as a quiet voice inside his head that helped him discern right from wrong. Thus Socrates equated his daemon with his conscience.

Daemons have gender in Pullman's universe. The gender is almost always the opposite of that of the character to whom the daemon is attached. This provokes several questions throughout the trilogy and becomes the catalyst for more than one incident. Not all of these incidents are suitable for the young audience.

One of the earliest incidents takes place in the bathtub. Lyra has left Jordan College, having been put into the care of Mrs. Coulter, a widow whom Lyra will later discover to be her mother. As Lyra strips off her clothing, her daemon Pan stares at her with what Pullman describes as a "powerful curiosity". Only when Mrs. Coulter glares at Pan does the daemon look away, following the example of the mother's daemon. Pullman describes this incident using the language of "modesty" and "feminine mysteries".

Obviously this incident plays some role in advancing the author's story line or ideas. *His Dark Materials* is a lengthy adventure in the fantasy genre— the focus is usually on action and fulfilling a quest. So why include a merely innocuous incident about bath time?

One need not be a literary scholar to interpret this incident. Pullman is raising the topics of gender and sexuality in the young reader's mind. While these are issues with which every Catholic will grapple as he enters adolescence, it is the responsibility of parents to guide their children's sexual development. It is not the task of children's fantasy authors. Children are, after all, impressionable creatures.

They are also naturally curious. Pullman has raised the question: What are these "feminine mysteries" of which he speaks, and why is no male pet permitted to look upon them? Especially since, in all other ways, the daemon is attached to the human character as a constant companion?

A second troubling incident arises when Pullman introduces a male character with a male daemon. The character is soon forgotten. He fulfills no other purpose in the trilogy; he is simply a character who shares the same gender as his daemon. Yet this is important enough for Pullman to note. Having raised the issue, Pullman then abandons the young reader to draw his own conclusions. The author's only explanation is that individuals who share their daemon's gender are rare, but they do exist. Once again, the child's curiosity is piqued, and he is left to grapple with the questions.

The third incident should prove by far the most troubling to Christian parents. By this time characters from Lyra's world have begun to interact with people from ours. The incident involves Dr. Grumman, a character from our world who has found himself trapped in Lyra's world. There he discovers the whole concept of daemons when his becomes external. He marvels at how people from our world cannot grasp a conscience that exists outside of the individual. They see their daemon as nothing more than a quiet voice inside their head. Dr. Grumman then expresses astonishment at the form his own daemon takes. It is a female osprey. Grumman concludes from this experience that one's daemon is part of one's nature. He states that part of his nature is female and formed like a bird.

The Bible is clear. God created us male and female. Our nature may be fallen because of original sin, but it is still human. Our nature is not female if God created us male, or male if God created us female. Thus Pullman's errors concerning human nature and the soul are a direct attack on Christian teaching.

Granted, many Christian thinkers have spoken of human beings of one gender possessing certain characteristics often associated with the opposite gender. The difference is that these writers never supposed that those traits indicated that one's soul is of the opposite sex. Pullman does. The daemons of his world have a definite gender, which is normally opposite that of the person to whom the daemon is attached, and the daemon's gender is tied to a person's human nature.

Poison Plots and Moral Relativism

Now back to Lyra hiding in the closet with her daemon Pantalaimon. While snooping upon the scholars of Jordan College, Lyra overhears a plot by the master of the college and the librarian to poison Lord Asriel. Those in on the plot expect Lord Asriel to ask for money to carry on his research, and they fear his research into experimental theology is attracting unwanted attention from the Church.

This is Pullman's first indication that there is something sinister about the Church because we are not sure why a legitimate university would fear the Church's attention. Pullman is not subtle about which Church he speaks. The Church in Pullman's world quotes Scripture, boasts cardinals and priests, and is referred to throughout the story as "the Magisterium". But more on that later.

The key danger here is the Church's different inquisitorial bodies. A conversation between the master and the librarian reveals a discomfort with their plot to poison Lord Asriel. Yet they feel no other option is available to them. They are fond of their adopted orphan, but the Church officials leading the inquisitorial bodies have some sort of vendetta against Lord Asriel.

The master and the librarian have hidden Lyra in Jordan College because she poses some sort of threat to the Church—a threat undisclosed at this point in Pullman's story. The plotters fear Lord Asriel's conflict may attract the Church's attention to Lyra, endangering the young orphan's life.

Thus the reader comes across Pullman's first use of moral relativism in the telling of his story. The master and the librarian were not truly evil in plotting to poison one of their colleagues. They were doing it for the orphan!

Now, Pullman never explicitly states that the master and the librarian were not acting with evil intention or that their actions were justified. Rather, he accomplishes this end in the way that he tells his story. He portrays the two plotters in a sympathetic light. There are no adverse consequences for so heinous a deed. The master and the librarian end up a little embarrassed, as their plot to stop Lord Asriel is foiled, but otherwise it is business as usual.

This last point is what separates Pullman from authors generally thought acceptable by Christians. Whereas the latter often depict characters as doing bad things, even doing bad things on the grounds of moral relativism, the characters do not go unpunished. Take C. S. Lewis' *The Lion, the Witch, and the Wardrobe*, for instance. For his treachery Edmund Pevensie must spend some time as the witch's prisoner before Aslan redeems him. Edmund, his siblings, and Aslan bear the consequences of his evil actions.

Similarly, Tolkien's Fellowship of the Ring is broken when Boromir forcefully attempts to take the

Ring of Power from Frodo. Boromir immediately repents of his evil; however, his action has attracted the attention of the orcs. Boromir is killed in the ensuing battle while defending Frodo's cousins Merry and Pippin. With Lewis and Tolkien, a character generally on the side of good is punished with serious consequences when he resorts to evil actions. With Pullman, the punishment is nothing more than a minor inconvenience.

Now, Catholic theology acknowledges that some laws do not apply when human life is threatened. For example, no Catholic would fault those German Christians who disobeyed civil authorities and used a certain amount of mental reservation or ambiguous language to hide Jews from Hitler's Nazi regime. However, as Saint Thomas Aquinas teaches, the end justifies the means only insofar as the means are consistent with the end being sought. In layman's terms, this means one can never resort to murder—or the unlawful taking of human life—to protect human life.

Is self-defense justifiable? Yes. But self-defense entails using that force necessary to repel an immediate and unjust attack against oneself or another. Self-defense does not entail a deliberate plot to poison another person who may pose some threat in the future. Thus the actions of the master and the librarian do not become morally irrelevant because of the uncomfortable situation in which they find themselves.

Regardless, the scholars' plot fails because Lyra overhears it. Lyra briefly finds herself alone with Lord Asriel. Unaware of the danger in which she will soon find herself, as well as the motive leading to the poisoning of the wine, Lyra reveals the plot to the man she believes to be her uncle.

At first he is angry—no female, let alone a child, is permitted to violate the sanctuary of the scholars' dining room. Lyra knows she is forbidden from entering the dining room; however, she has chosen to do so anyway. Upon determining that the plot is real and that Lyra is telling the truth, Lord Asriel relents on the condition that she remain in the closet. He wants her to spy for him while he gives his presentation to the other scholars. He orders her to watch the reaction of the poisoners when the wine is accidentally spilled.

This sends its own mixed message to children reading the book. It is another example of the situational ethics and moral relativism promoted by Pullman. A child is being told that it is okay to disobey rules and spy on other people if it benefits an adult to whom the child is related. The young reader will likely take this incident to mean that morality and obedience to rules are relative to the whims or interests of an adult.

Granted, Lyra did the right thing in alerting her uncle to the plot to poison him. She may have discovered this information while breaking the rules, but attempted murder is a serious enough action to warrant disclosing this information to a responsible adult. Yet the problem here lies with Lord Asriel. He is not a responsible adult. This is proven by his reaction to Lyra's revelation. A responsible adult would show concern for the child's welfare and remove her from the potentially lethal situation. Lord Asriel, on the other hand, puts her into the middle of it and forces her to spy on his would-be assassins.

This lack of responsibility is problematic because Lord Asriel is one of the story's main protagonists, and so his actions pervade the whole trilogy. The reader discovers near the start of *The Subtle Knife* that Lord Asriel is leading a rebellion against God, known as "the Authority". This is after Lord Asriel has sacrificed, at the end of *The Golden Compass*, the life of a child, a boy named Roger, who happens to be Lyra's best friend. Thus like many of history's revolutions, Lord Asriel's rebellion begins with the shedding of innocent blood. But more on that later.

The point here is that Pullman promotes situational ethics and moral relativism early on in his books. Lord Asriel is intended to be a sympathetic character. Pullman leads the young reader to believe that it is acceptable for an adult to recklessly endanger the life of a child in order to protect his own and, when the incident with Roger is taken into account, that it is permissible to murder a child in cold blood if in doing so one serves a higher purpose. This is moral relativism at its worst. No end can justify as its means the shedding of innocent life.

Now, in fairness to Pullman, he never comes out and says that Lord Asriel's actions are morally acceptable. However, neither is Roger's murder presented as immoral. Rather, Pullman leaves the young reader to wallow in ambiguity. Lord Asriel is never punished for the deed. Rather, his deed advances his war against the Authority. Thus the moral relativism, while not explicit, is strongly inferred.

Born of Adultery and Murder

Lord Asriel's actions become even more problematic when the reader discovers his true relationship to Lyra. He is not her uncle but her father. He has recklessly endangered the life of his own daughter, despite his natural obligation to nurture and protect her. The book ends with Lord Asriel killing

Roger, Lyra's best friend, to begin his war against God.

Returning to the beginning of the book, the Gobblers kidnap Roger and several other children. The Gobblers are an offshoot of the Church's inquisition. They are led by Mrs. Coulter, from whose care Lyra has just escaped. The Gobblers are holding the children captive in an Arctic research facility. Mrs. Coulter has also placed a bounty on Lyra.

Lyra is taken into hiding by the gyptians—a gypsy-like race of migrant boat people. They put her under the protection of an older gyptian woman named Ma Costa. This is somewhat ironic given Lyra's past—in an act of wanton hooliganism, Lyra had previously stolen and attempted to sink Ma Costa's houseboat. There was no end to justify this action; she simply harbored a prejudice against gyptians and thought it would be fun to sink the residence of one.

Several gyptian children have disappeared at the hands of the Gobblers. Thus the gyptian families, which follow a clanlike structure, gather to discuss the possibility of a rescue attempt. At this gathering Lyra meets with John Faa, the leader of the gyptian people. He has taken a special interest in the young girl. He tells her this interest goes back to her birth. From his lips Lyra (and the reader) learn about the violent circumstances surrounding her birth.

Lyra was conceived from an adulterous relationship between Lord Asriel and Marissa Coulter. Lord Asriel had earned a reputation as a daring young explorer, whereas Mrs. Coulter had married a close friend of the king. The adultery was nearly exposed with Lyra's birth; Lyra looked like her father. Mrs. Coulter, fearing for her reputation, turned Lyra over to a gyptian nurse who lived on one of Lord Asriel's estates. It just happens that the nurse was Ma Costa. Thus the beginning of the gyptian interest in Lyra's upbringing.

Mrs. Coulter wanted nothing to do with her illegitimate child. She pretended Lyra had died. Yet someone exposed the adultery to Coulter's lawful husband, who then sought revenge against Lord Asriel. The husband pursued Lord Asriel to his private estate. The explorer then turned around and killed his mistress' husband. The courts intervened, dispossessed Lord Asriel of his fortune, and gave custody of Lyra to a convent of nuns. Lord Asriel ignored the court order and turned baby Lyra over to Jordan College. He imposed one condition: the college can never give custody of Lyra over to her mother. Nevertheless, later Mrs. Coulter forces the college to give her custody of Lyra.

Lyra is barely shocked by the revelation that Lord Asriel is her father. Nor does she seem troubled by the fact that he happens to be an adulterer and a murderer. She accepts it. What horrifies her, however, is the discovery that Mrs. Coulter happens to be her mother.

One cannot change the circumstances of one's birth. Thus Lyra certainly deserves sympathy for being the offspring of a murderer and an adulteress. But once again, why raise these dark topics in literature aimed at children?

Christian parents must ask themselves why Pullman deems this material suitable for young audiences. Moreover, parents must ask why one of the characters involved looks heroic to Lyra—and through her, to the audience. Children are forced to grapple with the adult themes of adultery and murder committed by a character whom they are supposed to admire as one of the story's main protagonists.

Children face enough challenges to their innocence in today's world. Their minds need not be further darkened by Pullman's sordid plot lines and character development. Nor must they be confused by protagonists committing the darkest of sins.

Fomenting Rebellion against God

Lord Asriel and Mrs. Coulter will feature prominently in the unfolding of the plot. Near the end of

The Golden Compass, Lord Asriel murders Lyra's friend Roger to unleash the energy necessary to open a window to another world. The reader will eventually learn that Lord Asriel had requested a child for this experiment. He is shocked when Lyra, his own daughter, shows up. In fairness to Lyra, she confronts him about his unfatherly behavior. However, she will reconcile with her father and his mission by the next book.

Lord Asriel's rebellion against God is the most troubling aspect of Pullman's *His Dark Materials*. It forms the plot of the trilogy. However, Pullman does not reveal this to the reader until the beginning of the second book. Throughout *The Golden Compass* the reader is led to believe that the story centers around rescuing children from a masochistic Church. Following scripture that mimics the Christian Bible, the Church is on a fanatical quest to destroy Dust—something it believes to be the cause of original sin.

While Pullman has hinted in *The Golden Compass* that the Church was established by some sinister deity named "the Authority", he waits until *The Subtle Knife* to reveal fully how this piece of plot detail will affect the direction of the story. Lord Asriel does not seek to escape from the Church so that he may explore new worlds, as many—including the reader—are led to believe. Rather, he wants to confront the Authority directly and bring about his downfall. Lord Asriel is planning to kill the Authority.

This is the blasphemy central to the story's plot. This is why Lord Asriel murdered Roger—his daughter's best friend and an innocent child seeking solace from the Church during a harsh Arctic blizzard. This is what Hollywood, Pullman's publisher, and the American Library Association consider award-winning children's literature. Lyra and her friend Will—whom Pullman introduces in *A Subtle Knife* as a twelve-year-old boy from our world—will join Lord Asriel in his rebellion and bring about the downfall of the Kingdom of Heaven, and ultimately the Authority's death.

Yet some ambiguity remains within the second book as to the identity of the Authority. It would seem clear to the average reader. As previously mentioned, the Authority has established a Church similar to the Catholic Church in its structure, with its own scriptures that mimic the Christian Bible. Additionally, a connection has been made between the characters of Lyra's world and characters from our own. One of these characters from our world is Dr. Mary Malone, a former Catholic nun who previously abandoned her vocation in order to pursue science and sexual relationships.

Nevertheless, some still argue that Pullman is not talking about the Judeo-Christian God but a god created by man's dogmatism. One proponent of this idea is Rowan Williams, the Anglican archbishop of Canterbury. Williams has called for Pullman's work to be part of children's religious education.[1]

This theory becomes more difficult to maintain in *The Amber Spyglass*. In the trilogy's third book, a conversation ensues among Will, Baruch, and Balthamos. The last two are rebel angels of ambiguous sexual orientation who have joined Lord Asriel's revolt against the Authority. Will questions the angels about the Authority's identity, asking them whether the Authority is God. Keep in mind that Will is presented as an English child from our own world. Therefore, he likely shares the Judeo-Christian concept of God.

Balthamos answers Will's question as follows: "The Authority, God, the Creator, the Lord, Yahweh, El, Adonai, the King, the Father, the Almighty—those were all the names he gave himself. He was never the creator. He was an angel like ourselves—the first angel, true, the most powerful, but he was formed

[1] "The Dark Materials Debate: Life, God, the Universe . . .", edited transcript of a Platform at the National Theatre, *Telegraph*, March 17, 2004, http://www.telegraph.co.uk/arts/main.jhtml?xml=/arts/2004/03/17/bodark17.xml (accessed November 26, 2007).

of Dust as we are, and Dust is only a name for what happens when matter begins to understand itself." [2]

This is arguably the most dangerous passage in *His Dark Materials*. Pullman rejects God as revealed to us through Holy Scripture. He presents God as an angel who evolved out of preexisting Dust. Pullman calls God the first angel, a product of evolution who lied to the angels that followed. Thus Pullman leads the young reader to believe that God is a liar.

Against Pullman's lie stands the truth of Holy Scripture and Tradition. The Old Testament is clear: "God is not a man that He should lie", states Numbers 23:19. The First Vatican Council is similarly clear. It teaches that God can neither deceive nor be deceived.

Yet more dangerous than calling God a liar is the lie itself. The angel in Pullman's story asserts that God lied by falsely claiming to the other angels to be their creator. The only angel to see through this lie was an angel named Sophia (Wisdom). Yes, the devil is female in Pullman's fictional universe. "One of those who came later was wiser than he was, and she found out the truth, so he banished her", Balthamos tells Will. "We serve her still." [3]

---

[2] *The Amber Spyglass* (New York: Ballantine Publishing Group, 2001), 28.
[3] Ibid.

Why is this lie so dangerous to impressionable young readers? It contradicts the one article of faith from which the rest of our Catholic faith is derived, namely, that God in His omnipotence is the author of all creation. As Catholics we profess our belief in this truth each Sunday at Mass when we recite the opening of the Nicene Creed. "We believe in one God, the Father, the Almighty, maker of heaven and earth, of all that is, seen and unseen." God, omnipotent and eternally present, stands above creation.

Several heresies throughout the centuries have challenged the divinity of Jesus Christ. Few, save Lucifer himself, challenge that of God the Father. This is precisely what Pullman has done by identifying the Authority with the names by which God has been known in Holy Scripture. Pullman leaves little doubt in the young readers' minds that the Authority is the Judeo-Christian God.

Metatron, Seduction, and the Death of God

The Authority's identity is not the only revelation from the conversation that Catholics should find objectionable. The angels also disclose the identity of Metatron, the Authority's regent, who rules in his name. Metatron appears to be a synthesis of

Christ, Saint Michael, and a heavenly pope in terms of the functions he fulfills in *His Dark Materials*. Metatron is portrayed as the Old Testament prophet Enoch, who was taken to Heaven by God.

In Pullman's universe, once Metatron (Enoch) arrived in Heaven, he then became an angel and the Authority's closest advisor. God would delegate all His authority to Metatron in time and take on the life of a recluse. Metatron pursues Lyra, Will, Lord Asriel, and the rebel angels. To give their daughter and Will a fighting chance against the Authority, Mrs. Coulter makes seductive overtures toward Metatron. The angel states that he has not known a wife for several thousand years. Then he invites Lyra's mother to become his new consort.

Mrs. Coulter agrees. However, she has already chosen to betray Metatron to Lord Asriel. Together Lyra's parents bring about Metatron's death. They give their own lives in the process.

While this becomes a touching story of two parents who—after a lifetime of selfishness—sacrifice themselves for their daughter's sake, Pullman waters the seed of a dangerous metaphysic in the story's telling. Orthodox Catholic teaching holds that God created the angels as pure spirits. They cannot die. Nor can they be tempted by the sexual pleasures of the flesh. Yet this incident sets the stage for the

Authority's death in *His Dark Materials*. Contrary to the belief of many who have not read the books, Lyra and Will do not kill the Authority. He simply dies at their hands.

Lyra and Will discover a crystal into which the Authority has been captured and hidden away. He appears senile, fragile with age, and fearful of their presence. Pullman draws attention to the fact that the Authority—whom the author already established as the Judeo-Christian God—is "crying like a baby".

Lyra and Will open the crystal. The Authority attempts to smile. Then the strain proves too great for him in his weakened and demented state. He falls apart materially. God is dead in Pullman's universe. One need not go into much detail as to why Catholic parents ought to find God's death objectionable. Quite simply, God exists, in all His power, in an eternal present. He is not subject to time. Nor does He age.

Now, some will object that the Authority is not really God per se but a fraud purporting to be God. However, Pullman has given the Authority many of God's biblical names. Thus the young reader is led to identify the Authority with the Judeo-Christian God. Regardless of whether or not this is Pullman's intention, it is the interpretation to which the text of *His Dark Materials* most easily lends itself.

The Church, Dust, and Original Sin

"No servant is greater than his master", our Lord states in Saint John's Gospel (13:16). If Pullman's fiction ridicules God, Christians can expect to receive no better treatment at the end of Pullman's pen. Pullman caricatures the Church as an oppressive medieval institution that employs grotesque tortures similar to those of Chinese Communism.

The Church in *His Dark Materials* is obsessed with power. It exerts absolute control over the masses and gives its blessing to all types of evil action in the name of the Authority. Yet the Church in Pullman's world reserves its greatest cruelty for children.

This is seen in the reason Lyra and Roger had been seeking comfort and shelter with Lord Asriel. The two children had just escaped from Mrs. Coulter's Arctic laboratory, where the Gobblers took the children kidnapped by Mrs. Coulter. There, the children are measured, weighed, and subjected to scientific experiments. Once a child has been properly measured, Church scientists will place the child in a machine that severs the metaphysical link between child and daemon.

Most children do not survive the experiment. This is consistent with later passages in which Pullman establishes the daemon as part of a person's nature. Nevertheless, the Church feels justified in severing children from their daemons, which collect Dust when children become adolescents. Dust is only vaguely defined in *His Dark Materials*. It is believed to be matter that has become conscious of itself. Since Dust is thought to cause original sin in Pullman's universe, the author portrays the Church as severing children from their human nature in a fanatical attempt to save young people from the passions of adolescence.

Thus Pullman feeds off one of the oldest stereotypes perpetuated by the Church's critics. He is portraying the Church as anti-sex. While there is some ambiguity throughout the book as to how closely Dust is tied to intimate pleasures of the flesh, by the end of *The Amber Spyglass* there can be no doubt that Pullman links the two.

Any vagueness in the relationship between Dust, sexual attraction, original sin, and adolescence is resolved after God dies at the hands of Will and Lyra. Despite being from different worlds, the two twelve-year-olds begin to feel a deeper attraction for one another. Yet they are unable to act upon their passion until they figure out why Dust is disappearing from the world.

The reason Will and Lyra cannot act upon their budding romance is they have now come under the care of the *mulefa*, who are an alternate race of intelligent beings. The *mulefa* depend upon seedpods from the seedpod trees for transportation and survival. The disappearance of Dust is preventing the seedpod flowers from pollinating. Without seedpods, which resemble giant coconuts, the *mulefa* face extinction.

Throughout *His Dark Materials*, witches and other characters sympathetic to Lyra have prophesied her to be the new Eve. Dr. Mary Malone, the former Catholic religious, is told by shadow matter angels speaking through her computer that she must play the role of the serpent. Pullman portrays this as a good thing; however, Dr. Malone is not quite sure what this means. She also does not know where to find Will and Lyra. She turns to the occult—to divination—to find the young people. Malone is led on her journey by the ancient Chinese system of divination known as the I Ching. A vision will subsequently explain to the former nun how to play the serpent. She is to share her story with the young people about leaving the convent to pursue romantic relationships that involve cohabitation without marriage.

Pullman portrays this abandonment of a character's religious vows as a liberation rather than as a great tragedy. Dr. Malone's stories lead twelve-year-olds Lyra and Will to engage in passionate kissing as well as to sleep side by side under a hut, without the watchful eye of a responsible adult present. There is no explicit textual evidence that Will and Lyra engage in sexual intercourse; however, the situation lends itself to the young reader wondering. It is through this event that Lyra and Will renew the world of Dust and begin to repair the damage done. Their daemons become fixed, Will's having previously become external, and Will and Lyra engage in the petting of each other's daemons—an act of intimacy normally forbidden to another person. At the very least, the young reader is left to wonder about the nature of Will and Lyra's actions. There is no chance for marriage, as each must return to his world.

Of course the Catholic Church rejects Pullman's caricature of her teachings on sexual morality. The Church has great respect for the intimate life between husband and wife. "Be fruitful and multiply", states Genesis 1:26. In Ephesians 6:4, Saint Paul exhorts Christian fathers to raise their children with the discipline and instruction of the Lord. Obviously the Church does not oppose sex in all instances if she tells married couples to bear children and raise them in the Lord.

What the Church opposes is sex divorced from its natural openness to new life as well as from the stability of marriage and the family. This is to protect husband, wife, and any children born of the union. Lyra's parents are the perfect example of what happens when sex is divorced from the context of marriage and the family. The adultery is the source of grief for all three parties.

Pullman and the Church's Cruelty to Children

But back to *The Golden Compass* and the Church's cruelty to children. Most children do not survive the severing of their daemon. Those who do survive find themselves in a state of shock—outcasts, alone, and missing part of their nature. The Church does not care for its victims. It tosses them into the Arctic climate to fend for themselves. Because people in Lyra's world cannot conceive of a person without a daemon, these children are shunned as horrors when they stumble upon an Arctic village. Most children do not make it far without their daemon. They either freeze to death, or they starve.

Additionally, throughout the trilogy, Church officials lie, confiscate property, and engage in petty infighting. When it comes to the treatment of children, priests and other agents of the Church torture, murder, kidnap, and mutilate them—the mutilation being both physical and metaphysical at different points in the story.

The Church even dispatches a priest to carry out a mafia-style hit against Lyra. The priest is a member of one of the Church's more zealous sects, and he attempts to carry out the hit with the full blessing of the Church. In fact, the Church grants the hit-man priest preemptive absolution. This means the priest receives God's forgiveness for killing Lyra prior to carrying out the act.

Unfortunately, not all Catholics are properly catechized, and thus this error could well resonate among readers. In truth, the Church could never sanction preemptive absolution for sins one is about to commit. After all, one of the conditions of a valid confession is the penitent's firm purpose of amendment. This means the penitent approaching absolution is firmly resolved to sin no more. This is the exact opposite of what Pullman suggests in his dark parody of the Church.

Thus Pullman's portrayal of the Church as cruel to children is merely a caricature. In reality, the Church loves children and defends human dignity. A cursory reading of the *Catechism of the Catholic*

Church will show any sincere person that the Church believes abortion is a grave evil (2271), that murder is the intentional and direct taking of innocent human life and a violation of the fifth commandment (2261), and that torture is contrary to the respect due to each person (2297).

What makes Pullman's caricature dangerous, however, is the point of history in which we find ourselves. The Church is recovering from a sexual abuse crisis. This crisis arose because many children were harmed by Church officials who did not remain faithful to Church teaching and to their sacred vows. The Church's enemies have also spread many misconceptions about Pope Pius XII and the role of the Church in facing down Hitler during World War II. So while non-Catholics and young people would probably reject Pullman's caricature, the temptation is to see it as an exaggeration rather than as a falsehood. This is one reason why Catholic parents must be vigilant.

Christianity Itself Is Oppressive

Likewise, our Protestant brothers and sisters should be wary. Pullman's caricature of the Church includes them. In Lyra's world, the Protestant reformers remained within the Church, elected John Calvin to the papacy, and moved the Church's headquarters to Geneva. They then did away with the papacy altogether. So while Calvinism has influenced the Church's theology in this alternate world, the institution retains most of the external trappings of Catholicism.

This too is a dangerous error concerning the Church's divine foundation. It is probably too subtle for most young people consciously to pick up on, but Pullman is telling the reader that theological differences among Christians are meaningless. What matters most to the Church—as Pullman's alternate history of the Counter-Reformation leads young people to believe—is power and how to assert it over the masses. This is Karl Marx's old canard that religion is the opium of the masses. Pullman has repackaged it for mass consumption by unsuspecting youth and their parents.

Moreover, by making Calvin the pope and having the Church subsequently abolish the papacy, Pullman intends his readers to see both Catholic and Protestant Christianity as flawed and harmful to humanity. Furthermore, although Pullman's Church has certain Catholic elements to it, Protestants can take little comfort from that, since Pullman's attack on the God of the Bible is hostile to Protestant belief as well as to Catholic Christianity.

The Christian Martyrs, Pullman's Afterlife, and the Death of the Soul

The zealots even remain zealots in Pullman's portrayal of the afterlife. It is a gloomy Limbo-type atmosphere that resembles the Greek Hades rather than the Christian Heaven and Hell. Every soul goes there after death. It does not matter whether the soul lived a life in accordance with God's grace or not. All souls go to the same place, where they wait indefinitely.

Lyra encounters several souls of what appear to be Christian martyrs during her time in the afterlife. She and Will have come to rescue their friend Roger. Pullman first appears to poke fun at Catholics by singling out a soul that resembles a monk. The zealous monk desperately tries to convince the other souls trapped with him that the gloom and doom is in fact the glory of Heaven.

Pullman singles out souls of martyrs and saints for the opposite reason. They feel betrayed. They had given their lives to serve God and the Church, hoping for the promise of Heaven. They complain that the Authority misled them. There is neither Heaven nor Hell, no final judgment to separate the sheep from the goats. Everyone goes to the same gloomy place.

These are the circumstances in which Pullman transforms Will and Lyra into a mockery of Christ. Will and Lyra suffer by giving up their daemons to visit the afterlife, much like Christ suffered on the cross. Lyra strikes a bargain with the harpies, a demonlike race that occasionally tortures the souls in the afterlife by using knowledge of their sins. The bargain struck, Will uses the subtle knife—a knife of magical properties after which the second book is named—to cut a hole out of the afterlife. The task now falls upon Will and Lyra to lead the souls out of the afterlife, much like Christ descended into Hell to free the souls of the Old Testament and lead them to Heaven. Only there is no Heaven for the souls in Pullman's story. Once outside of the afterlife, these souls dissolve into Dust to be recycled into the atmosphere.

Thus Pullman's eschatology, whether intentionally or not, mocks that of the Christian faith. He appears to mock the martyred saints, who witnessed for Christ and His Church with their blood. He also appears to mock the eternal afterlife professed by Catholics and other Christians, Christ's descent into Hell, and the permanence of the soul. One can infer from this that Pullman also rejects the bodily resurrection, since in his portrayal of the afterlife the soul eventually dissolves like the body.

Christian parents have the right to be outraged over the marketing of these ideas to children. It undermines our fundamental faith in redemption and eternal salvation.

The Occult

As the reader no doubt has become aware, Pullman often mocks the Catholic Church and her leaders. The author takes a different tack when introducing the occult. He presents witches and shamans as the true spiritual leaders of his multi-verse (as opposed to uni-verse) which includes our world and other alternate worlds. These witches and shamans are important supporting characters. Without their assistance, Lyra, her parents, and Will could not organize and perpetuate the war against the Authority.

The magic in *His Dark Materials* is not like the elf-magic of Tolkien. In *The Lord of the Rings*, elf-magic is pure fantasy. It belongs to a special race and is used to create objects of some value. In contrast, Pullman's use of magic is occult. The most obvious example is the golden compass, the magic item after which the first book is titled.

The golden compass' rim is surrounded by different symbols rather than numbers. Each of these symbols represents a category of meaning, which then descends into different levels of meaning. Thus a sheet of paper might represent an important document, a letter, or a book. The golden compass is also referred to by the characters as an "aleithiometer"—that is, a truth measurer. It is a form of divination. Its power comes from angels structured from shadow matter who intervened in human evolution out of vengeance. The user sets three of the compass' arms, focuses upon a question, and then watches as the compass' fourth arm swings to various symbols. The user then interprets the answer. Both good and evil characters make use of the aleithiometer for their ends.

A second example of Pullman's use of divination arises with Dr. Mary Malone, the nun from our world who lost her faith in God, left the convent, and became an experimental scientist in search of dark matter, which is referred to as Dust in Lyra's world. She discovers the capacity to communicate with dark matter when she turns to the Chinese form of divination, I Ching. It is through the I Ching that the former nun helps rescue Lyra and Will. Dr. Malone also has a computer through which she communicates with the angels structured from shadow matter. It is through this computer that she is told by the dark angels to play the role of the serpent. The message to young readers is obvious. The occult can succeed in helping one do good, whereas the

Judeo-Christian God will only disappoint or lead one to do evil.

The example of Lord Asriel's sacrificing Roger has already been noted. Lord Asriel murders an innocent child to unleash the energy necessary to open a portal between worlds.

Against this use of the occult, Holy Scripture is clear. God condemns both divination and child sacrifice. "There shall not be found among you any one who burns his son or his daughter as an offering, [or] any one who practices divination", states Deuteronomy 18:9. Thus Pullman's use of magic is not neutral, a literary device used to move the story forward; it openly defies Christian belief.

A Parent's Obligation

Parents are their children's primary educators. In fact, canon 1055 of the Church's *Code of Canon Law* states that the procreation and upbringing of children is one of the essential ends of marriage. Young couples marry with the intention of bearing and raising children. The Church understands the education of children as not only academic but also as ensuring that children's physical, emotional, and spiritual needs are met. A tribunal can declare a marriage invalid if a party attempts marriage without intending to provide for a future child's education.

Thus Catholic parents need to be aware of the spiritual and intellectual dangers that *His Dark Materials* poses to their children. Pullman is no Inkling in the tradition of Tolkien and Lewis who uses magic and fantasy as a literary device to promote a Christian worldview. The opposite is true. Pullman has intentionally written *His Dark Materials* as a rebuttal to Lewis' *Chronicles of Narnia.* He borrows Lewis' Narnian imagery, with which many children are familiar. Pullman then inverts Lewis' imagery and uses it both to attack the Christian worldview and to promote atheism.

Thus Catholic parents should think carefully before allowing their children to read Pullman's books. And parents whose children have already read the books should take whatever time is necessary to discuss their contents. Keeping children spiritually grounded is one of a parent's most important obligations. Christ, who told his apostles, "Suffer the little children, and forbid them not to come to me: for the kingdom of heaven is for such" (Matthew 19:14), also said, "It were better for him, that a millstone were hanged about his neck, and he cast into the sea, than that he should scandalize one of these little ones" (Luke 17:2).

Finally, Christians can pray for the conversion of Philip Pullman. He too is a child of God in need of Christ's healing touch and salvation. Whereas Pullman may have turned his back on God, our Lord has not turned his back on Pullman. "I say to you, that even so there shall be joy in heaven upon one sinner that doth penance, more than upon ninety-nine just who need not penance" (Luke 15:7).

What about the Movie?

Should Catholic parents allow their children to see the movie, which reportedly has been stripped of its anti-Catholic and anti-Christian imagery? The recommendation of this author is no.

Christ states very pointedly in Matthew 7:18: "A good tree cannot bring forth evil fruit, neither can an evil tree bring forth good fruit." The movie is the fruit of the books and Pullman's imagination. These are anti-Christian and atheistic at their core. And in any case, however modified the film may be, it is still a two-hour commercial for the books, which have not been toned down; they remain saturated with atheism and an anti-Christian agenda. Why open Pandora's box with your child's soul? It is better simply to ignore the movie, like most Christians did with the pro-homosexuality cowboy flick

Brokeback Mountain, or use the movie release as an opportunity to discuss the importance of faith and culture with one's children.

Finally, a boycott is not a picket. In picketing Dan Brown's *The Da Vinci Code*, many well-intentioned Christians ended up drawing more publicity to the film. Already certain individuals who share Pullman's atheistic worldview are trying to provoke a similar reaction among Christians with respect to *The Golden Compass*.

Ignore the bait. Freedom of speech works both ways. Pullman may enjoy the right to promote his blasphemy as children's literature, but freedom of speech also means Christians have the right to remove themselves from speech they find offensive. Catholics are under no obligation to pay Hollywood and the publishing industry to insult their faith. Thus the advice of this author can be summarized as this: "Stay home, but do not picket."

Children face enough challenges to their innocence in today's society. Let us not expose them to Philip Pullman, the pied piper of atheism.

Chapter 2

The Darkness of His Materials

Sandra Miesel

Philip Pullman is a gifted writer. His prose is graceful, his imagination rich, and his powers of observation keen. Nevertheless, Pullman is dangerous, for he instills atheism through his artful stories—while primly claiming not to do so.

Pullman's trilogy, consisting of *The Golden Compass* (1995), *The Subtle Knife* (1997), and *The Amber Spyglass* (2000), takes its overall title *His Dark Materials* from a line in John Milton's *Paradise Lost*. In *Paradise Lost*, the term refers to the formless substance of the primeval abyss, the "dark materials" of past and perhaps future creation. Satan ponders this on his way to tempt Adam and Eve. In *His Dark Materials*, Pullman argues for a revolution to remodel the cosmos. An egalitarian Republic of

Heaven will replace the dictatorial Kingdom of Heaven, once the imposter calling himself God the Almighty Authority is destroyed.

Pullman devised his own myth to explain the state of the universe, declaring that the wrong side won the original war in Heaven. The rebel angels' cause was just because the Authority was not the Creator but merely the first angel to coalesce from particles of consciousness called Dust. His tyranny provoked a futile rebellion led by a female angel named Sophia (Wisdom). Although the counterfeit god and his loyal angels prevailed, the vanquished retaliated by intervening in evolution everywhere in the universe. They gave all sentient creatures the self-awareness and wisdom that the Authority did not want them to have.

For Pullman, the ancient Gnostic heretics were right: the serpent of Eden helped rather than hurt Adam and Eve. The loss of innocence is a necessary step toward maturity. The Fall of man should be a cause for celebration—it is a "happy" event, not a "fault" at all. And in this topsy-turvy view, the Fall most certainly did not merit "so great a Savior" in the person of Jesus Christ, as the Easter Vigil liturgy proclaims.

Gnosticism was a bubbling brew of Christian, Jewish, and pagan ideas that flourished in the early centuries of Christianity. From the Gnostics' confused teachings comes Pullman's rejection of the biblical God. Pullman specifically identifies his Authority as Yahweh, God's Old Testament name, in *The Amber Spyglass*. Knowledge saves by exposing this God as a finite, created usurper. In some interviews, Pullman gives an unconvincing nod to the remote possibility of some ultimate Divine Principle somewhere but has seen no evidence of it himself.[1] In others, he has indicated that if a real God somehow exists, such a Being "deserves to be put down and rebelled against".[2]

There is neither a Gnostic "spark of the divine" in Pullman's characters, however, nor a sharp distinction between "good" spirit and "evil" matter. The characters say that "matter and spirit are one." Both are destined for the same noble fate: to be recycled into the substance of the universe. People will live fuller lives and die cheerfully once they realize that there is no Heaven, no Hell, nothing beyond this horizon. People will feel "free" when

[1] Steve Meacham, "The Shed Where God Died", *Sydney Morning Herald*, December 13, 2003, http://www.smh.com.au/articles/2003/12/12/1071125644900.html (accessed November 29, 2007).

[2] Interview on the BBC's *Breakfast with Frost*, January 27, 2002, http://news.bbc.co.uk/2/hi/programmes/breakfast_with_frost/1785121.stm (accessed November 29, 2007).

they no longer believe in the supernatural. Kindness and understanding will flourish once the coercive Kingdom of Heaven is overthrown. The victory of natural virtues in a godless cosmos of frank materialism is perhaps Pullman's most fantastic notion.

Pullman was greatly inspired by the visionary Romantic poet William Blake, especially by his *Marriage of Heaven and Hell*. Blake shared Pullman's distaste for organized religion as repressive hypocrisy "binding with briars my joys & desires".[3] Both writers also consider the "improvement of sensual enjoyment"[4] to be redemptive. Blake, who thought that angels and devils should have their labels reversed, wrongly claimed that Satan was the hero of *Paradise Lost* and that its author, Milton, "was of the Devil's party without knowing it".[5] Pullman, of course, blithely admits that he himself is in the Devil's corner. He reads Milton through Blake's eyes as well as his own.

According to the *Catechism of the Catholic Church* (*CCC*) (327–30), angels are pure spirits, personal and immortal, instantly created by God out of nothing at the beginning of time to be His servants and messengers. The *CCC* quotes Saint Augustine: "If

[3] William Blake, "The Garden of Love", line 12.

[4] William Blake, *The Marriage of Heaven and Hell*, plate 14, line 7.

[5] Ibid., plate 6, Note.

you seek the name of their nature, it is 'spirit'; if you seek the name of their office, it is 'angel': from what they are, 'spirit,' from what they do, 'angel.' " Pullman dares to borrow Saint Augustine's definition as his rebel angels' self-description—flashing across a computer screen in an Oxford laboratory.

As a Christian, Milton believed angels to be direct creations of God, whereas Pullman depicts them as gradually condensing from consciousness after matter had begun thinking about itself. But not being a Catholic, Milton followed the Neoplatonist theories of his time, which viewed all spiritual beings as corporeal. His angelic bodies are hard to see but wonderfully swift, and capable of shrinking, swelling, and transforming their appearance or sex at will. They can even eat, something Pullman's angels do, too.

The "subtle bodies" of Pullman's angels are winged, sexually equipped, and—as in Jewish lore—mortal. Nevertheless, Pullman coyly insists that the relationship between his homosexual angels is strictly Platonic because their angelic bodies are too delicate for sexual activity. In contrast, Milton's angels are male in grammatical gender only, not in their actual anatomy. They are able to express their amorous attachments by dissolving into each other's being as a "union of pure with pure" (*Paradise Lost*, 8.618–29).

Pullman's angels, however, feel lust and envy, the sensory possibilities of human flesh. As in the apocryphal books of Enoch and the Book of Jubilees and in some occult sources, they can mate with human women and raise humans to angelic status. Genesis 6:2–4 mysteriously mentions the *bene elohim*, the "sons of God" (meaning "divine beings", not literal offspring) who begot the "mighty men who were of old" (the Nephilim) through human wives. But Pullman uses the term *bene elim*, or "sons of gods", from Psalm 29:1.

Although Pullman's angels can live for many thousands of years, they do age, decay, and feel pain. Since the first rebellion more than thirty thousand years ago, the proud Authority has become helpless and senile. He is now confined within his celestial palace, called the Clouded Mountain or the Chariot (Merkabah), a concept borrowed from Jewish mysticism. Pullman has the audacity to say—and to have a leading character say—that the Old Testament itself records the aging of God from Genesis to Daniel, because He appears in the latter book as the white-haired Ancient of Days (Daniel 7:9). Apparently Pullman cannot recognize symbols and metaphors as figurative language.

The Authority has surrendered power to his regent, Metatron, who was originally the man

Enoch, who lived seven generations from Adam. Pullman's Metatron is a ruthless dictator bent on directly controlling all life. Historically, occultists call Metatron the Prince of the Divine Presence, so powerful and glorious that he is easily confused with Almighty God. This gigantic spirit of fire, equipped with seventy-two wings and 365,000 eyes, is also known as the King of Angels, Prince of this World, and the Lord's Chancellor. Metatron dominates the apocryphal three books of Enoch, which describe dazzling celestial splendors and may be among Pullman's sources.

But in Genesis 5:24, "Enoch walked with God" and was taken out of the world while still alive. He and the prophet Elijah are traditionally identified as the two witnesses who return to die at the end of the world in Revelation 11. Some occultists say that Elijah was turned into an angel named Sandalphon, who conveniently happens to be the twin brother of Metatron.

Both magic and science work in Pullman's trilogy because the mystical and the material are one. Spirit loves matter in his monistic universe. Matter somehow arose out of nothingness, evolved to a point where it could start thinking about itself, then generated the particles of consciousness called Dust, which condensed into angels, who raised the consciousness of intelligent beings, whose wisdom and creativity create more Dust to enhance further perfection. Pullman presents a sort of cosmic perpetual motion machine driven by purely natural causes.

In one part of Pullman's universe, theoretical physics is "experimental theology" that must explore within the standards of orthodoxy—or face heresy charges. Where the iron fist of organized religion does not interfere, magic and science collaborate. A physicist and a witch pledge sisterhood; a shaman's spell propels a gas balloon; a blacksmithing bear repairs a tool made by alchemists. The mystical and material come together most elegantly in the third novel's amber spyglass, which is a rudimentary scientific instrument that can see the elusive beauty of Dust.

Pullman relies on the familiar science-fictional premise that a multitude of parallel worlds invisibly coexist in the universe, generated by branching pathways of chance and choice. His characters move among several of these through windows cut in the space-time fabric by "the subtle knife" called "God-destroyer". The concept of parallel worlds is hardly novel. H. G. Wells first used it in "The Strange Case of Davidson's Eyes" (1895). It was firmly embedded in American pulp fiction conventions before World War II.

Pullman indicates the differences among his worlds cleverly enough, for instance by changes of terminology ("anbaric" for "electric") or by political references (Imperial Russia still in conflict with the Tartars). But the historical nexus points implied would not plausibly lead to the results shown. For instance, his America, where Viking settlements succeeded and Indians adopted European culture, could not produce a classic Texas cowboy in the twentieth century. An England whose technology is mostly Edwardian is most unlikely to have advanced knowledge of nuclear physics or be able to work titanium.

The Golden Compass introduces Pullman's twelve-year-old heroine, Lyra Belacqua. She lives in an alternate Oxford that is contemporary with ours and is dominated by a grim analog of the Catholic Church called "the Magisterium". It has priests and nuns, and bishops in purple and cardinals in red, but no pontiff because Pope John Calvin moved the Vatican—complete with crossbow-wielding Swiss Guards—to Geneva where the papacy was later abolished. The Church's rival bureaucracies harshly control life over much of the globe, crushing natural impulses, sniffing out sin, and hunting heretics. It tortures and executes those who oppose it. The Magisterium teaches that original sin is an acquired, rather than an inherited, condition. It plans

to keep future generations innocent by psychic mutilation. Christ—and therefore redemption—is curi-
ously absent from its creed.

Like all humans in her world, Lyra has a personal
daemon, one named Pantalaimon (All-Merciful).
This is an externalized psyche in talking animal form
that is changeable for children but stable for adults.
Ordinarily, daemons are opposite in sex to their
humans. (The rare exceptions are presumably homosexual.) Daemons live and die with their humans,
manifesting the humans' inner essence. Humans
forcibly severed from their daemons lose their imagination and free will. But witches and others who
have borne the pain of voluntary separation gain
unique powers.

Lyra's adulterous parents, furious Lord Asriel and
sinister Mrs. Coulter, have a snow leopard and a
golden monkey for their daemons. Unappealing cler-
ical daemons include a snake, a lizard, a frog, and a
beetle. Humans in our world also have daemons,
although they usually cannot see them. The daemon
is the soul (*psyche*), the ghost is the spirit (*pneuma*),
and the body is the flesh (*sarx*), corresponding to
the ancient Greek theory of human nature.

Daemons express their humans' true character.
A bold person might project a lion but a timid one a
poodle. Although they are a gift of the rebel angels,

they are no more diabolical in themselves than Jiminy Cricket in Walt Disney's *Pinocchio*. The daemon—known to Milton as an "Attendant Spirit"—is Pullman's most charming invention. He created them by crossing ancient Greek concepts of spiritual guardians and counselors with folklore about animal familiars and totems. Unfortunately, they are the feature most likely to attract children to *His Dark Materials*.

At the start of the trilogy, Lyra is a wild and heedless girl erratically educated by Oxford scholars—and an accomplished liar. The golden compass, called an "aleithiometer" (truth meter) in the book, is a clockwork oracle through which the rebel angels communicate. After Lyra learns to read it by instinct, it guides her on a quest to the Arctic to rescue her favorite playmate Roger and other missing children. She is aided by gyptians (gypsylike boat people), a cowboy balloonist named Lee, a Finnish witch-queen named Serafina, and a talking armored polar bear named Iorek.

The kidnapped children are saved from monstrous scientific experiments run on behalf of the Magisterium by Lyra's mother, Mrs. Coulter. Iorek kills a rival to regain his throne. Lyra's father, Lord Asriel, plots a new revolt against God. He sacrifices Lyra's friend Roger to blast an opening between parallel worlds. Lyra follows him into the breach. (The film cuts the finale of the book.)

The Subtle Knife opens in our Oxford, where twelve-year-old Will Parry discovers a window into an alternate world. He steps into an Italian-looking city, where Lyra is hiding, and they become friends. He wins the subtle knife that can slice through anything, even the fabric of the universe. Back in Will's Oxford, Lyra meets sympathetic physicist Dr. Mary Malone, an ex-nun who has spurned her faith. Meanwhile, Lyra's mother has learned that Lyra is prophesied to be the new Eve and kidnaps her.

Lyra is being held captive by her mother at the start of *The Amber Spyglass*. Helped by two homosexually bonded angels, Will escapes Mrs. Coulter's wiles and rescues Lyra. Will and Lyra are aided by a pair of gallivespians—miniature, dragonfly-riding humanoids with venomous spurs on their heels. The Magisterium plans to destroy Lyra while Lord Asriel prepares to attack God, the Authority, now recognized as a senile imposter. Using the subtle knife, Will and Lyra break into the land of the dead, a shadowy prison where the ghosts of all sentient beings are tormented by harpies. They free the ghosts for blissful extinction in sunlight.

During the final Armageddon assault, Lyra and Will unwittingly destroy the feeble Authority, who is relieved to be put out of his misery. Her parents hurl Heaven's regent Metatron into the abyss— along with themselves. Clinging together, this unholy trinity will fall forever toward nothingness yet never die.

Lyra and Will rejoin Mary in a primitive paradise where religion has never intruded upon its kindly, peaceful, artistic native race, called the *mulefa*. Mary plays the serpent and awakens the children to desire. They kiss, and it is implied that they make love. This reverses the flow of Dust back into the universe, and the cosmos is saved. But the survivors must return to their home worlds to build the new god-free Republic of Heaven.

True to form, Pullman is coy about his climax. He dismisses analysis of Lyra and Will's amorous behavior as improper curiosity. "Nowhere in the book do I talk about anything more than a kiss", he told the *Sydney Morning Herald* on December 13, 2003.[6] Nevertheless, the last chapters of *The Amber Spyglass* are filled with lush, erotically charged imagery that suggests much more than the words say. Pullman invests innocent words such as "little", "soft", "sweet", and "gentle" with insidious sensuality. The simple gesture of putting food in

---

[6] Meacham, "Shed Where God Died".

another's mouth becomes a sign linking the Fall and sexual experience. In Pullman's Gnostic-inspired scheme, this is the beginning of wisdom. In her role as Tempter, Mary mirrors what the chief rebel angel Sophia and her followers did for all intelligent beings.

Christianity has traditionally taught—and the Catholic Church still teaches—that the sin of Adam and Eve was disobedience. Nevertheless, a certain association between the primal sin and intercourse still lingers in the popular imagination, hence the connotations of "forbidden fruit". But the opening lines of *Paradise Lost* announce the sin's content: "Of Man's first disobedience and the fruit / Of that forbidden tree, whose mortal taste / Brought death into the world and all our woe". Furthermore, Milton had described Adam and Eve already enjoying marital embraces in Paradise and, unlike Lyra and Will, staying together after they are banished. As a Christian poet, he really was of God's party and not the Devil's.

Despite his public avowals of atheism, Pullman was shrewd enough to maintain deniability. After all, the Authority is a mere "metaphor", not *really* God. The children are trying to *help* him, not hurt him. In a November 5, 2007 article in the *Christian Post*, Pullman is quoted on his self-satisfaction at killing God "as a result of an act of charity".[7] One minor character does acknowledge that the existence of a real Creator is unknown. Although witches denounce all churches as enemies of joy and truth, Pullman's text implies that their pagan gods are also illusionary. (What a suffering witch imagines is her goddess of death is merely a fellow witch.) The only religious figures who receive honest respect are a Siberian shaman and a Buddhist monk.

The Magisterium has specific trappings of Romanism, yet former Anglican Pullman claims that it stands for faith perverted by power and zealotry, not the actual Catholic Church. Nevertheless, Pullman told the Readerville Forum in February 2001 that "I was trying to hit a target worth hitting" because of disgust at reports about "brutal monks" and "sadistic nuns" harming children.[8]

Pullman spoils his art with unrelenting bias. From the fanatical leader who throws his life away trying

[7] Katherine T. Phan, "'Golden Compass' Author Denies Promoting Atheism in Books", *Christian Post*, November 5, 2007, http://www.christianpost.com/article/20071105/29957_'Golden_Compass'_Author_Denies_Promoting_Atheism_in_Books.htm (accessed November 29, 2007).

[8] "Philip Pullman in Readerville", Readerville Forum, February 5–9, 2001, http://www.readerville.com/webx?14@992.cCpKas87yrZ.1@.ef6c70e/0 (accessed November 29, 2007).

to destroy Lyra to the vulgar Russian priest who plies Will with vodka, all Pullman's clerics are crude stereotypes worthy of a Jack Chick tract. They are variously power-mad, cruel, lecherous, cowardly, drunken, and deceitful. The last of the lot is a gaunt Spanish assassin who is armed with preemptive penance and absolution for his mission to kill Lyra. He might as well be a skulking Jesuit hunting Queen Elizabeth. But instead of being martyred at Tyburn, the priest is drowned by an effeminate angel, and a lizard feeds him to her young.

The Golden Compass film tries to block religious controversy by avoiding the word "Church" and defining the Magisterium as "the councils that form the heart of the government in Lyra's world". (Nevertheless, in an MTV interview on November 14, 2007, director Chris Weitz indicated that this tactic merely prepares the way for more faithful adaptations of *The Subtle Knife* and *The Amber Spyglass*.)[9] Pullman himself has softened his tone in recent promotional appearances. On the *Today* show for November 21, 2007, he denied that his books push

[9] "'Golden Compass' Director Chris Weitz Answers Your Questions: Part I", MTV Movies Blog, November 14, 2007, http://moviesblog.mtv.com/2007/11/14/golden-compass-director-chris-weitz-answers-your-questions-part-i/ (accessed November 27, 2007).

an atheist agenda,[10] yet he had told the *Washington Post* six years earlier, "I am trying to undermine the basis of Christian belief."[11] Meanwhile, in Britain, the National Secular Society has denounced the film's changes for blunting the books' message, and disappointed readers vent their displeasure on fan websites.

Pullman preaches against religion through dialogue between characters previously established as trustworthy in the text, yet he claims that he is not responsible for what they say. When ex-Catholic nun and atheist Mary Malone dismisses Christianity as "a very powerful and convincing mistake", is agreement between her opinion and Pullman's own a mere coincidence? Although scenes of torment inflicted by obvious villains—agents of the Magisterium—do not imply that Pullman approves of torture, are all those leading characters who rejoice at being recycled back into nature contradicting their author's views? What of suicide? Is it justified for a feeble old man or a bereaved angel?

[10] "Pullman Not Promoting Atheism in 'Golden Compass'", *Today*, November 2, 2007, http://today.msnbc.msn.com/id/21595083/ (accessed November 27, 2007).

[11] Alona Wartofsky, "The Last Word", *Washington Post*, February 19, 2001, http://www.washingtonpost.com/ac2/wp-dyn/A23371-2001Feb18?language=printer (accessed November 27, 2007), p. C01.

Is euthanasia permitted when an injured witch begs for it or forbidden when a crippled toad does not? Are life and death merely matters of choice? Pullman's readers could easily be led to that conclusion.

Sympathetic critics hail Pullman's "daring" as if atheism were a novelty. "The books make a breath-takingly subversive attack on organized religion and on the notion of an all-powerful god", said Sarah Lyall in a *New York Times* article.[12] But science fiction master Fritz Leiber's *Gather, Darkness* had the counterfeit god, corrupt theocrats, feisty witches, bad angels, and satanic freedom fighters—back in 1943. Wicked priests and false cults have long been a staple of the popular adventure genre, as any reader of Robert E. Howard or any *Star Trek* viewer knows. Even Pullman's egalitarian rejection of the King-dom of Heaven was anticipated—at least as a metaphor—in the 1988 treatise *God's Federal Repub-lic* by William Johnson Everett.

Pullman's most sustained attack on God the Authority and his Church comes in *The Amber Spy-glass* when Lyra and Will free all the dead of all the

[12] Sarah Lyall, "Staging the Next Fantasy Blockbuster", *New York Times*, January 25, 2004, http://query.nytimes.com/gst/fullpage. html?res=9B05E2D91239F936A15752C0A9629C8B63 (accessed November 27, 2007).

worlds from imprisonment in endless gloom. The ghosts are not confined in Milton's Hell but in a place closer to Blake's "land of sorrow & of tears where never smile was seen".[13] By the Authority's cruel command, there is neither reward for virtue nor punishment for vice, only a barren plain of clay like the biblical Sheol. Here, as a Miltonic touch, classical harpies harass the shadowy dead. (Pullman picks harpies of woman-headed bird designs and loads them with disgusting details.)

Agonizing separation from their daemons is the price of admission for the living, and the subtle knife opens the prison door. Lyra finally learns to stop lying after a harpy attacks her for doing so. She pacifies the chief harpy with a true story, later embraces her, and names her Gracious Wings. (Madeleine L'Engle's heroine finds a similar solution with a foe in *A Wind at the Door* [1973].)

The harpies agree to release the dead in exchange for their life stories. Will cuts an exit, and the ghosts flow out to see life for one last moment before popping like happy bubbles of champagne. Because ghosts, like angels, have a tenuous material quality, the particles of their being will disperse everywhere into nature.

---

[13] William Blake, *The Book of Thel*, part iv, line 5.

Reabsorption into the cosmic All, like a drop of water returning to the sea, is the fulfillment promised in pantheism, but Pullman is a sentimental materialist. Why would scattered atoms of an individual retain any memory of the living person, considering that they would have passed through innumerable different people over the ages? As consolation for separation and death, this is cold comfort indeed.

By annihilating the dead, Lyra and Will have destroyed death. This is the greatest blow anyone has yet struck against the Authority. The whole adventure is an attack on Christianity's beliefs about the afterlife. A martyr in Pullman's land of the dead regrets sacrificing her life for a lie. But a monk insists that the Church's lie was true and that—to the eyes of faith—their dismal fate is really celestial glory. He fancies he has achieved the goal of Milton's Satan: to make of Hell a Heaven.

Pullman emphasizes that no one of any species ever returned from the land of the dead. Christ's Resurrection is not even worth a specific denial, and, of course, He never harrowed Hell. Pullman says that leading ghosts to extinction is better than releasing souls from bondage in Limbo so they can have joy in Heaven. (Similarly, Ursula K. LeGuin undermines belief in personal immortality and clears out a comparable Underworld in her National Book Award winner *The Farthest Shore* [1972].)

Pullman builds subversive meanings into his characters' roles and names. Lyra's identity as the long-prophesied new Eve makes her a blasphemous double of the Virgin Mary, for that is how Saint Justin Martyr described our Lady around A.D. 150. Lyra's original family name, Belacqua, means "beautiful water" in Italian. Her mother's first name, Marisa, is an Italian diminutive of Mary. (Outrageously, a symbol of the Madonna represents Marisa in a reading of the golden compass.) Lyra's friend Dr. Malone, the ex-nun, is also called Mary, a name of uncertain history that has been variously interpreted as "beloved", "beautiful", "bitter", "long awaited", "bride of the sea", "drop of the sea", and the inaccurate but favorite title among Catholics, "star of the sea" (*stella maris*), which is attributed to Saint Jerome.

Thus Lyra, Marisa Coulter, and Mary Malone stand for the three phases of a woman's life, or to Pagans, the three faces of the goddess: Maid, Wife/Mother/Mistress, and Crone. But Lyra as the new Eve repeats the deed of the old Eve, instead of reversing it as the sinless Blessed Virgin Mary did. Marisa's smothery mother-love for Lyra is a form of possessiveness that makes her no more nurturing toward others. Her marriage and her love affairs are for expedience and pleasure. Led away from religious life by carnal desire, Mary is no longer sexually active, yet she knows how to make erotic experience attractive to others. (The original Mother Eve advised her to do it by telling stories.) Mary's role as the serpent in an alien Eden recalls the feminine features of the Tempter in much medieval and Renaissance art.

To complement the above, Lord Asriel's silvery leopard daemon is named Stelmaria (Star Mary). (In medieval bestiaries, the leopard stood for Satan as the deceiver.) Lord Asriel is a satanic figure, complete with an angelic name "Asriel" means "Vow of God" but in occult lore, he is sometimes confused with Azrael, the angel of death.

Lord Asriel plays Samael (Poison of God) to Marisa's Lilith, the demonic temptress and enemy of children. Fiery Samael, prince of demons and a magician, was the adversary of Metatron, though he trembled at his sight on first meeting. (Pullman could have possibly expanded his resonances to make Asriel an angel-turned-human, the reverse of Metatron.) Samael supposedly was the true father of Cain by Eve, and Lilith had been Adam's abandoned first wife. Samael and Lilith were also married to each other, and both have serpentine elements in their legends.

Marisa's married name, Coulter, refers to the steel edge of a plow. "The cut worm forgives the plow" is one of Blake's "Proverbs of Hell".[14] But do the eggs forgive the omelet maker? Are Marisa's vicious deeds offset by her giving help to Asriel in assaulting the regent of Heaven? Oddly, Marisa Coulter's golden monkey daemon is not named, and his communications with his human go unrecorded. Because she starts out in *The Golden Compass* as an ardent follower of the Magisterium, her loathsome monkey may have been inspired by a revolting passage in Blake's *Marriage of Heaven and Hell* that likens churchgoers to monkeys who rape and devour one another. Pullman's moral principle that there are only good and evil deeds, not good and evil people, seems to have been drafted with Marisa and Asriel in mind. But that would also exonerate churchmen and other villains in the trilogy.

Asriel and Marisa are masculinity and femininity pushed to almost impossible extremes. The cloying prettiness of Marisa's London home stands against Asriel's dark fortress in the North. As adulterous lovers, they play Mars and Venus to her late husband's Vulcan, except that Asriel fatally shoots jealous Edward Coulter.

---

[14] Blake, *The Marriage of Heaven and Hell*, "Proverbs of Hell", line 6.

But Will and Lyra enact less conventional gender roles, despite his symbolically masculine knife and her feminine compass. He is introverted and nurturing and hates violence, while she is an extroverted, scrappy leader. He knows how to cook and keep house; she does not. Although Will is a necessary partner in their adventures, Lyra is the dominant figure, perhaps to redress what Pullman sees as sexism in past fantasies. Will stands for the human will learning about freedom; Lyra represents the human intellect learning about truth.

While not exactly magical, their artifacts, the knife and the compass, operate at the borders of observable reality. The knife was made by alchemists in Cittàgazze, the City of the Magpies, on another world more than three centuries earlier (coincidentally in the same year that Milton copyrighted *Paradise Lost*). The experimenters were trying to slice matter into its smallest components but produced a knife that could cut portals into other worlds. Like thieving magpies, they used it to steal indiscriminately. But portals left unclosed let in bits of the primal abyss called Specters that suck out adults' psyches, leaving them in a zombielike state. (Pullman could have applied his fine talents to dramatizing the perils of technology, but he chose to attack religion instead.) Will wins the subtle knife in personal combat—at the cost of two fingers, the sacrifice required of knife bearers. At one point, the knife is broken and reforged, as fantasy heroes' swords so often are.

Lyra's "truth-measuring" golden compass, an exquisite Baroque ouija board, sends messages via thirty-six pictorial symbols instead of twenty-six letters. It was made in 1700 in Prague, a city famous for alchemy in our world. Lyra must drop into a special state of concentration to read its messages from the rebel angels, just as Will must do to use the knife.

The passage from *Paradise Lost* that Pullman quotes at the opening of *The Golden Compass* describes the primeval abyss, from which all things came and to which they may return. The classical four elements of water, earth, air, and fire roil within it, unable to mix yet fighting for mastery. Pullman's characters correspond to these elements. Their enmities and alliances drive the action according to principles laid down by Aristotle. Lyra is fire (hot and dry); Will is earth (dry and cold). Her parents reverse the polarity, so Asriel is fire and Marisa is earth. The angels, Lee the Texas balloonist, and the witches are air (wet and hot); Iorek, his polar bears, the gyptians, and the Jordan College staff are water (cold and wet), and so on through the cast. Allies fire and earth are extremes, but their paired opposites, air and water, are blends. Earth is contrary to air, and fire to water, but earth bonds with fire, and air with water. Thus, Will and Lyra are drawn to each other, while Lee and Iorek become close friends.

These patterns would have been thoroughly familiar to C. S. Lewis because of their importance for studying Western literature. Yet despite some common intellectual interests, Philip Pullman is the antithesis of C. S. Lewis. "He is the anti-Lewis," says British writer Peter Hitchens, "the one atheists would have been praying for, if atheists prayed".[15] Those who love Lewis as a scholar, artist, evangelist, and Christian gentleman find Pullman's smug atheism a blight on children's literature. But secularists who deplore the Christian themes of Lewis' Narnia series consider Pullman their Great Dark Hope for immunizing the young against faith. Unbelief is so much more "sophisticated", so much more deserving of literary awards. Note that although both Lewis and Pullman won the Carnegie Medal for children's fiction in Britain, Pullman's *Amber Spyglass* received the Whitbread Book of the Year prize there competing against adult novels. Hitchens quotes Pullman's

[15] Peter Hitchens, "This Is the Most Dangerous Author in Britain", *Mail on Sunday*, January 27, 2002, http://www.home.wlv.ac.uk/~bu1895/hitchens.htm (accessed October 5, 2007).

judgment: "I hate the Narnia books, and I hate them with a deep and bitter passion."[16] Did that declaration win Pullman important friends?

It is no accident that Lyra begins her adventures in *The Golden Compass* hiding in a huge oak wardrobe— just as Lucy does in *The Lion, the Witch and the Wardrobe*. (There are even fur coats in both places.) Both Lewis and Pullman got the inspiration for their series from isolated mental images. Both populate their worlds with talking animals and mythical species. Both use children as protagonists. But while Lewis rejected any suggestion of romance between children, Pullman makes it the centerpiece of his trilogy.

Lewis, a specialist in medieval and Renaissance literature as well as a reader of fantasy and science fiction, respected the genre in which he worked. His friend George Sayer observed, "The Narnia stories liberated the children's story from its bondage to realism." Pullman, on the other hand, does not like or understand fantasy. He rejects that label for his books, for, to him, only "stark realism" is truthful. (Besides despising Narnia, Pullman dismisses J. R. R. Tolkien's *Lord of the Rings* as "infantile".)[17]

[16] Ibid.

[17] Laura Miller, "Far from Narnia", *New Yorker*, December 26, 2005, http://www.newyorker.com/archive/2005/12/26/051226fa_fact?currentPage=5 (accessed November 29, 2007).

So deep is Pullman's aversion to Lewis that he marked the hundredth anniversary of Lewis' birth in 1998 by viciously denouncing the man and his work in Britain's premier leftist newspaper, the *Guardian*.[18] Pullman's essay ran a month before the paperback edition of *The Subtle Knife* appeared.

In the essay, Pullman mocks the well-known facts of Lewis' life as hagiographic "legend". His hottest wrath is directed at the Narnia series, "one of the most ugly and poisonous things I've ever read". Sadly, his "open-eyed reading" is simply blind.

A few examples will suffice. Pullman, who expects his readers to see Will and Lyra as the new Adam and Eve, cannot recognize Aslan as a genuine Christ figure for Narnia. He charges Lewis with sexism, yet Lucy—modeled on a girl Lewis knew—is the character with the purest heart. Digory, not Polly, rings the fatal bell that sends sin into Narnia. Edmund succumbs to the White Witch, and Eustace to selfishness, until Aslan intervenes. And as for disinterest in women during his Narnia-writing years, Lewis first made contact with his future wife, Joy Davidman, in 1950, the year that *The Lion, the Witch, and the Wardrobe* appeared,

---

[18] Philip Pullman, "The Dark Side of Narnia", *Guardian*, October 1, 1998, http://www.crlamppost.org/darkside.htm (accessed October 5, 2007).

and married her in 1956 when the final volume was published.

Pullman accuses Lewis of sending Susan to Hell in *The Last Battle* merely for wanting to grow up. But Susan is neither damned nor a participant in *The Last Battle*. How did Pullman see a girl who does not appear in person in the book? Bedazzled by his theory that Lewis was afraid of adulthood, Pullman does not notice that the characters do age across the span of the series; some even marry and grow old. The original four siblings from *The Lion, the Witch and the Wardrobe*—who spent years as adult rulers in Narnia—are past puberty and out of school on earth by the start of *The Last Battle*.

The conclusion of that final book, when Aslan brings his now deceased faithful Narnians to Heaven, enrages Pullman. He calls it "one of the most vile moments in the whole of children's literature".[19] He will not suspend his (literal) disbelief and accept this as a happy ending under the conditions in the story. To him, "it's propaganda in the service of a life-hating ideology." He would prefer to see characters live with maximum intensity and cheerfully accept personal oblivion at death. Disguise it as he may with false charges,

[19] Ibid.

Pullman's key objection is Lewis' Christian faith, which he attacks as "a religion whose main creed seemed to be to despise and hate people unlike yourself".[20]

Ironically, Pullman accuses Lewis of "a sadomasochistic relish for violence".[21] Yet his own novels offer gore far more graphic than anything in Narnia. Pullman sees no reason to shield young readers from harsh realities. Besides battles, he also dramatizes murder, suicide, mutilation, torture, euthanasia, and cannibalism. Iorek the polar bear eats his fallen rival's heart and his best friend Lee's corpse. Specters destroy human personality by devouring daemons. Living animals are tormented or torn apart for sport. Will has learned to inflict pain on playground bullies and has to kill some of the feral children hunting him and Lyra in a pack. Yet Pullman complains about the "loathsome glee" of Narnian heroes who rout a mob of nasty schoolmates in *The Silver Chair*—though they inflict no lasting harm.

Both married and unmarried characters have love affairs in Pullman's books. Lyra was conceived in adultery, followed up by homicide. Will's father is

---

[20] Dave Weich, "Philip Pullman Reaches the Garden", Powell's Books, August 31, 2000, http://www.powells.com/authors/pullman. html (accessed November 27, 2007).

[21] Pullman, "Dark Side of Narnia".

murdered for spurning a witch's love. Priests show an unhealthy interest in children. Mrs. Coulter is more mendacious, manipulative, and murderous than any witch of Narnia. She stirs the most powerful angel in Heaven to white-hot lust. She unleashes Specters against a former mistress of Lord Asriel and personally poisons one of her own lovers. Erotic play between her monkey daemon and the dying man's snake daemon is a singularly disturbing scene to set before middle-school readers.

Some Christian critics trained their heavy artillery on J.K. Rowling instead of on Pullman, who hit the market first. This amuses Pullman greatly. "Harry Potter's been taking all the flak", he told the *Sydney Morning Herald* in 2003. "Meanwhile, I've been flying under the radar, saying things that are far more subversive than anything poor old Harry has said. My books are about killing God."[22]

Witches abound in the Harry Potter series, as do wizards. Magic abounds. Releasing the first volume in America as *Harry Potter and the Sorcerer's Stone* (instead of the *Philosopher's Stone* of the British original) rang alarm bells. But, Rowling's magic is a natural, inborn ability, not Gnostic "secret wisdom". Her unique incantational spells invoke no gods or

---

[22] Meacham, "Shed Where God Died".

demons and require no elaborate ceremonies. Her magic is an alternate form of technology that other humans cannot use.

In contrast, Pullman's Arctic witches come from lines in Milton—with a glamorous twist. Beautiful, strong, pagan, sexually permissive, and passionately connected with nature, they embody modern Wiccan dreams. The long (but ultimately unsuccessful) healing ritual shown in *The Subtle Knife* broadly resembles Neopagan ceremonies. Divination, via the golden compass or the I Ching or a computer program, is reliable in Pullman because it transmits messages from the "truthful" rebel angels. But Rowling ridicules divination class and pities its pathetic teacher.

Redemptive sacrifice and other Christian themes weave through the seven Harry Potter books. As John Granger has ably demonstrated in his book *Unlocking Harry Potter*, Rowling's intricately structured series is based on alchemy: spiritual dross is transmuted into spiritual gold. (The Narnia books may have also used the alchemical mystique of planets and their metals, according to scholar Michael Ward.) Pullman's myth borrows a bit of Gnosticism to spice up his materialism. He celebrates the Fall of man, the liberating loss of innocence, and personal extinction in a godless cosmos. The saga of Harry Potter culminates in fruitful, happy marriages, but Lyra and Will must part at the end of *His Dark Materials*. Which writer's vision is more hopeful?

Like Lewis, Rowling and Pullman understand the power of storytelling to instruct as well as delight. (Pullman has a brilliant style, but if he had matched Rowling's mastery of narrative misdirection, he could have evangelized for atheism without overt preaching.) Pullman's recent soothing disclaimers that he is only "telling a story"[23] need to be corrected by comments from past years. As Peter Hitchens quoted him saying in 2002, "All stories teach, whether the storyteller intends them to or not. They teach the world we create. They teach the morality we live by. They teach it much more effectively than moral perceptions and instructions.... We don't need lists of rights and wrongs, tables of do's and don'ts: we need books, time, and silence."[24]

Who wants Philip Pullman shaping children's worldviews and values with *His Dark Materials*?

Suggested Reading

Blake, William. *The Marriage of Heaven and Hell.* Available in many editions.

[23] Phan, "Author Denies Promoting Atheism".
[24] Hitchens, "Most Dangerous Author".

Brown, Nancy Carpentier. *The Mystery of Harry Potter: A Catholic Family Guide.* Huntington, Ind.: Our Sunday Visitor Press, 2007.

Granger, John. *Unlocking Harry Potter: Five Keys for the Serious Reader of All Seven Books.* Wayne, Penn.: Zossima Press, 2007.

Kilpatrick, William, et al. *Books That Build Character: A Guide to Teaching Your Child Moral Values Through Stories.* New York: Simon and Schuster, 1994.

Lewis, C. S. *An Experiment in Criticism.* Cambridge: Cambridge University Press, 1965.

——. *Of Other Worlds.* Edited by Walter Hooper. 1975. New York: Harcourt, 2002.

——. *A Preface to Paradise Lost.* New York: Oxford University Press, 1942.

Milton, John. *Paradise Lost.* Available in many editions.

Silvey, Anita, ed. *Children's Books and Their Creators: An Invitation to the Feast of Twentieth-Century Children's Literature.* Boston: Houghton Mifflin, 1995.

Tolkien, J. R. R. "On Fairy-Stories". In *The Monsters and the Critics, and Other Essays.* Edited by Christopher Tolkien. London: HarperCollins, 1997.

Zipes, Jack, ed. *The Oxford Companion to Fairy Tales: The Western Fairy Tale Tradition from Medieval to Modern.* New York: Oxford University Press, 2000.

Appendix A

Tales of Wonder for Today's Children

Sandra Miesel

Families who told stories around the fire long ago did not know that they were laying the foundation of literature, much less children's fantasy. But the gift to imagine and organize one's imaginings in an enjoyable narrative is a major step on the road to civilization. Tales of what might have been and what might yet be nourish the human spirit by taking us beyond the fields we know. All fantasies do this, but children's fantasies do it in particularly pure and potent form.

Historically, children's fantasies grew out of fairy tales. These bubbled up from the Great Cauldron of Story when writers repackaged popular oral traditions about magic, monsters, and myth for elite audiences to read. Fairy tales were first published in sixteenth-century Italy, but the ones that directly influenced our culture were written for adults at the court of Louis XIV in France. Charles Perrault's classic versions of "Sleeping Beauty", "Cinderella", "Puss in Boots", and other tales were printed in English in 1729 and came to be called "Mother Goose stories".

But during the Enlightenment, high-minded people were suspicious of fairy tales as children's fare. Whether driven by reason or faith, parents wanted children to read only "improving" books, nothing more fantastical than *Aesop's Fables* or nursery rhymes. In 1817, a magazine reviewer decreed that "works of fancy highly wrought . . . we would not put into the hands of young people till their religious principles are fixed."

Nevertheless, Perrault and other French authors continued to sell editions designed for children. When the tenor of the times turned Romantic, whatever was primitive or exotic or fantastic became fashionable. The fairy tales of the Brothers Grimm, supposed to have been gathered from peasant storytellers and afterward touched up for literary effect, were eagerly received in English translation in 1825–1826. A generation later, Hans Christian Anderson's fairy tales also became popular. Major Victorian writers, including John Ruskin and Oscar Wilde, wrote original literary fairy tales. Lewis Carroll (*Alice in Wonderland* [1865]) and George MacDonald (*At the Back of the North Wind* [1871]) showed that children's fantasy could escape the fairy tale form.

But the very popularity of fantastic fiction deluded some people into believing that it was uniquely suited for simple young minds—and only young minds. Fantasy was turned into a vehicle for moralizing or lethally whimsical stories that talked down to children and had nothing to offer adults. Art, however, was not extinguished. Early twentieth-century writers such as Edith Nesbit, Rudyard Kipling, and Kenneth Grahame penned works that can still be read with pleasure by all ages. L. Frank Baum produced the first American fairyland in his Oz books.

The great fantasy breakthrough of the twentieth century was J. R. R. Tolkien's "subcreation" of a secondary world for his children's novel *The Hobbit* (1937) and its mature companion *The Lord of the Rings* (1954–1955). A secondary world is fully developed, commanding the suspension of disbelief, allowing the reader to enter a thoroughly convincing imaginary realm. The intricate detail of Tolkien's Middle-earth, with its own languages, species, geography, history, and cultures, has never been equaled.

The American paperback publication of *The Lord of the Rings* in 1965 started a boom in both adult and children's fantasy that continues to this day. Fantasy books regularly take the top prizes for children's literature. The best children's fantasies cannot be dismissed as mere "kid lit". Their grace and beauty have enduring appeal—even to adults. As C. S. Lewis says, "A children's story which is enjoyed only by children is a bad children's story." And a book that seems coarse or badly written to an adult is unworthy of a child. Sausage-link commercial series and media spin-offs offer no lasting value for any age.

Contemporary children's fantasy still returns to its roots by retelling traditional fairy tales and folk tales. For example, Madame Leprince de Beaumont's "Beauty and the Beast" (1756) was given a romanticized treatment and an eighteenth-century setting by Robin McKinley in *Beauty* (1978), but Nancy Willard transferred it to a robber baron's mansion in the Hudson Valley for her *Beauty and the Beast* (1992), and Andre Norton took the story to another planet in *The Year of the Unicorn* (1965). Contrarian retellings are also popular, such as the humorous parodies in *The Stinky Cheese Man, and Other Fairly Stupid Tales* by Jon Scieszka (1992), in which the protagonist of "The Gingerbread Man" is made of Limburger.

Fantasy critic and editor Mike Ashley divides the children's fantasy genre into six types. Here are his categories summarizing the kinds of premises used in children's fantasy, plus classic examples.

1. *Worlds in miniature* feature tiny beings or animated toys. *The Borrowers* by Mary Alice Norton (1952) depicts miniature humans who live behind the walls of homes, and *The Indian in the Cupboard* by Lynn Reid Banks (1980) brings a toy to life.

2. *Secret gardens* are enchanted realms reachable from our world. Frances Hodgson Burnett's *Secret Garden* (1911) is a fantasy only in mood, but *Tom's Midnight Garden* by Philippa Pearce (1958) is an intriguing refuge in the past.

3. *Time fantasies* are concerned with travel backwards, forwards, or sideways in time. L. M. Boston's Green Knowe novels (1954–1976) gather children from different generations who lived in a country house. *The Devil's Arithmetic* (1988) by Jane Yolen transports a contemporary girl back to the Nazi Holocaust. Joan Aiken's James III series (1962–1995) take place in an alternate version of England. Rosemary Sutcliff's Arthurian trilogy (1980–1982) dramatizes a magical past.

4. *Other worlds* are complete secondary worlds. C. S. Lewis' *Chronicles of Narnia* (1950–1956) and

J. R. R. Tolkien's stories of Middle-earth are benchmarks of this type.

5. *Wish fulfillments* use magical artifacts, as in Edith Nesbit's *Five Children and It* (1902), or trace the emergence of a magical talent, as in *Archer's Goon* by Diana Wynne-Jones (1984).

6. *Animal stories* can show humanized animals in the manner of Rudyard Kipling's *Jungle Books* (1894–1895) or use them in fables, as in his *Just So Stories* (1902). The thinking rabbits in Richard Adams' *Watership Down* (1974) are naturalistic, but Beatrix Potter's dressed animals are the finest of their kind.[1]

What are the good fruits of reading fantasy? J. R. R. Tolkien's famous essay "On Fairy-Stories" describes some qualities of that genre that can be extended to fantastic literature in general—fantasy, recovery, escape, and consolation. *Fantasy* means the art of "subcreation", a human analogue of God's creativity that gives invented worlds "the inner consistency of reality". *Recovery* means the "regaining of clear view" so that we see the universe as it truly is. *Escape* frees the reader from the ugliness of modern life and man's estrangement from nature. The

[1] Mike Ashley, "Children's Fantasy", *The Encyclopedia of Fantasy*, eds. John Clute and John Grant (New York: St. Martin's Press, 1997), 184–89.

traditional happy ending offers *consolation* for it denies "universal final defeat" and gives a glimpse of ultimate joy.[2]

Children's fantasy is implicitly spiritual because it tells the truth about right and wrong. Catholic journalist Eve Tushnet points out its potential as an antidote to cultural poisons and as a means of pre-evangelization. By breaking away from ego stroking in the here and now, fantasy speaks more clearly to readers' pain than scab-picking "problem novels".[3] It encourages moral growth and confidence in a universe that somehow makes sense. Each reader is rehearsed for a hero's role, invited to make the long quest and slay the dragon so the world may be healed. What fantasy fictionalizes, salvation history makes real, for all of us are characters in God's very own story.

[2] J. R. R. Tolkien, "On Fairy-Stories", *The Monsters and the Critics*, ed. Christopher Tolkien (London: HarperCollins, 1997), 107–61.

[3] Eve Tushnet, "Outside Narnia: Children's Fantasy and Christianity", *Crisis*, July 2, 2002, http://www.crisismagazine.com/julaug2002/feature5.htm (accessed December 11, 2007).

Appendix B

Reading Recommendations

Sandra Miesel

In addition to the works mentioned in Appendix A, here are some tried and true fantasies, chosen to show a variety of types. Series are given by overall title. Because books go in and out of print, only the year of publication is given. For out-of-print books, try ⟨www.amazon.com⟩ or ⟨www.bookfinder.com⟩.

Early Readers / Read Aloud

Fairy tales are essential. Try Oxford's *Classic Fairy Tales*, edited by Iona and Peter Opie (1974), or Pantheon's *Folktales of the World* series (1963–1979), edited by Richard Dorson. Judge individual picture book editions by the quality of the art. The best artists and writers work together.

Barklem, Jill, author and illustrator. The Brambly
   Hedge series. 1980–1994. Dressed mice in the
   British countryside for the youngest readers.
Eager, Edward. *Half-Magic.* 1954. Humorous adventures with a magic coin. The next six books in
   the series are not quite as good.
Steig, William, author and illustrator. *Sylvester and
   the Magic Pebble.* 1969. Curious donkey gets
   enchanted. Almost anything by Steig is delightful.

Middle Readers (Ages 9–12)

Alexander, Lloyd. *The Chronicles of Prydain.* 1964–
   1967. Adventures in a fantasy kingdom like medieval Wales.
Briggs, K. M. *Hobberdy Dick.* 1955. Country folk
   magic in Cromwell's England.
Chesterton, G. K. *A Father Brown Reader.* Edited
   by Nancy Carpentier Brown. 2007. Introduces
   Chesterton's mysteries for middle-school readers.
Garner, Alan. *Elidor.* 1965. The Holy Grail hidden
   in Manchester. His *Owl Service* (1967) is for mature
   readers only.
Goudge, Elizabeth. *The Little White Horse.* 1946.
   Magical environment in Regency England. Also
   try her *Linnets and Valerians* (1964).

Hoban, Russell. *The Mouse and His Child*. 1967. Toy mice want to become self-winding.

Jacques, Brian. Redwall series. 1989–. Medieval dressed animal adventures. The series has 18 volumes as of 2007. His Flying Dutchman series is also good (2001–).

Norton, Andre. *Octagon Magic*. 1967. Enchantments through needlework. Her time-travel fantasy *Red Hart Magic* (1974) and American Indian animal fantasy *Fur Magic* (1968) are also good. *Lavender-Green Magic* (1974) is not recommended.

Wynne-Jones, Diana. Chrestomanci series. 1977–1988. Alternate world of magic.

Young Adults (Teens)

Anderson, Poul. *Three Hearts and Three Lions*. 1961. Danish hero in alternate world of magic. *A Midsummer's Tempest* (1974) combines Shakespeare and the English Civil War.

Bellairs, John. *The Face in the Frost*. 1969. Comedy and horror in a magical alternate world.

Benary-Isbert, Margot. *The Wicked Enchantment*. 1955. Magical impersonation in Catholic Germany.

Lowry, Lois. *The Giver*. 1993. Mystical answer to futuristic tyranny. The sequel, *Gathering Blue* (2000), is also excellent.

McKinley, Robin. *Rose Daughter*. 1997. Exquisite retelling of "Beauty and the Beast". Her *Deerskin* (1993) and *Sunshine* (2003) are strictly adult fare.

Pope, Elizabeth Marie. *The Perilous Gard*. 1974. Fairy folk in Tudor England.

Preussler, Otto. *The Satanic Mill*. 1971. Fighting Satan in early modern Germany.

Wrede, Patricia. *The Enchanted Forest Chronicles*. Boxed set, 2003. Comic fantasy about tomboy princess and dragons.